CLEANING UP
A COMPUTER MESS

A Guide to
Diagnosing and Correcting
Computer Problems

CLEANING UP
A COMPUTER MESS

A Guide to
Diagnosing and Correcting
Computer Problems

William E. Perry

 VAN NOSTRAND REINHOLD COMPANY
New York

Library of Congress Catalog Card Number: 85-3271
ISBN: 0-442-27491-2

Manufactured in the United States of America

Published by Van Nostrand Reinhold Company Inc.
135 West 50th Street
New York, New York 10020

Van Nostrand Reinhold Company Limited
Molly Millars Lane
Wokingham, Berkshire RG11 2PY, England

Van Nostrand Reinhold
480 Latrobe Street
Melbourne, Victoria 3000, Australia

Macmillan of Canada
Division of Gage Publishing Limited
164 Commander Boulevard
Agincourt, Ontario M1S 3C7, Canada

15 14 13 12 11 10 9 8 7 6 5 4 3 2

Library of Congress Cataloging in Publication Data

Perry, William E.
    Cleaning up a computer mess.

    Includes index.
    1. Electronic data processing departments — Management.
2. Debugging in computer science.   I. Title.
HF5548.2.P47279   1985   658'.054   85-3271
ISBN 0-442-27491-2

*To my wife Cindy, who never understood what a
computer mess was until I bought her a home computer
to help her do her work*

PREFACE

One of the greatest agonies in life is to be responsible for a technical device that won't work — and you don't know how to fix it. The feeling of frustration and helplessness is without comparison. The computer is the ultimate technological device that, when broken, appears to defy all laws of correction.

The only real solution to computer problems is to build application systems right the first time. The short-term solution is to adopt a process for identifying problems, diagnosing the cause, and then having a shopping basket full of solutions to use. The purpose of this book is to provide that corrective process.

Computer mess solutions included in this book have been developed at great cost by the pioneers of data processing. In the process, some managers lost their jobs, some businesses turned over their data processing to service bureaus, but others survived and went on to create and solve more problems. This book is dedicated to helping make you a survivor of the computer wars, not a casualty.

WILLIAM E. PERRY

CONTENTS

CLEANING UP
A COMPUTER MESS

A Guide to
Diagnosing and Correcting
Computer Problems

Part 1
So Now You Are in Trouble

When the bubble of naiveté bursts and you realize the management commitment and corporate resources required to make a computer tick, you will probably be mired in a computer mess. Fortunately, you will not be the first one there. Recognizing the problem is the first step toward a solution.

1
HOW DOES A COMPUTER MESS ORIGINATE?

Cheer up, my friend, life could be worse; so I cheered up, and sure enough, it got worse.

Any highly advanced technology is almost indistinguishable from magic. The computer surely qualifies as advanced technology. There is little doubt that to many people the computer is magic. After all, hasn't this technological wonder enabled men to go to the moon? But we must not forget that, at the same time, the computer has fouled up charge accounts so miserably that it takes an army of accountants to straighten out the mess.

The computer has been known to humble the strongest of men. It is a sad sight to watch a grown person cry as a deadline clicks nearer moment by moment while the computer does nothing to help. That machine called a computer does nothing more, or nothing less, than what it has been instructed to do.

Visualize for a moment your arrival at an unknown location. Although you have been given instructions on how to get to your appointed destination, you are lost. The trip started out well, but quickly disintegrated as you failed to recognize any of the designated landmarks. The more you attempted to find your way or retrace your steps, the more lost you became. Eventually, the situation appeared to be hopeless, so you stopped, uncertain of where to proceed. If you can picture that situation, perhaps you can sympathize with a computer that has been improperly instructed. It becomes hopelessly lost and covets help, but at that low point in the life of the computer, the operator asks directions. How can the computer help a lost soul when it too is stymied at the end of a dead-end street?

The solution to any problem begins with the recognition that there is a problem. Too frequently, people hope that the next bend in the road will point the way to their destination. Unfortunately, the next bend normally leads only to the next bend, which leads to the next.   Slowly, those people begin to dig themselves into a hole that is difficult to get out of.

History tends to repeat itself in installation after installation. The same type of mistakes made by Company A are made by Companies C, D, E, F, etc. Because experience is such a valuable teacher, let's see what we can learn from the costly data processing mistakes of the last twenty-five years.

THE COMPUTER USAGE CYCLE

One of the primary characteristics of a manual processing environment is *unpredictability*. About the only thing a manager can depend upon with people is that they may not do the same thing the same way twice. Therefore, to manage and control a manual processing environment, we build controls to address unpredictability. These include segregation of functions, division of duties, redundancy of processing, and checking and inspecting work.

The common characteristic of a computerized business environment is *predictability*. The computer will do the same thing the same way every time — right or wrong! This is why it is possible to pay every employee wrong on the same payday, produce hundreds of bad invoices in a matter of minutes, or destroy an entire file as quickly as it can be read. Controls that work in a manual environment may not be effective in a computerized environment.

The same predictability can be applied to the installation and operation of a computer. Almost all installations go through the same computer cycle. Unfortunately, many people in business fail to recognize the existence of the cycle and the pitfalls inherent in it. Therefore, those businesses pay an avoidable high cost to relearn what thousands of other businesses have already learned.

The use of the computer in business follows three steps — from simple to sophisticated. This computer cycle passes through the following three steps of computer technology usage, which are illustrated in Figure 1 and explained below:

- *Step 1: Using computer technology for major accounting systems.* Upon acquiring a computer, most organizations place their major accounting systems on the computer. These are the major bread-and-butter applications of the business, such as

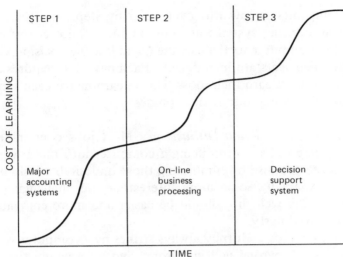

Figure 1. Computer usage cycle.

payroll, accounts receivable, inventory control, sales, etc. These systems tend to have high volumes with minimal processing complexity. Many organizations can purchase predeveloped software packages to handle these mainstream accounting applications.

- *Step 2: Using computer technology for on-line business processing.* This use of technology permits the users to interact with the computer in the performance of their jobs. For example, an order entry clerk can check the status of inventory prior to processing an order, or a bank teller can directly update an account while the transaction is being processed. In the previous use of technology, the users prepared data for and received data from the computer. In this use, the users are the computer operators, and the computer is an essential part of their jobs.

- *Step 3: Using computer technology for decision support systems.* This use of technology is for management. The previous two uses were for the day-to-day production worker or office worker. The types of information produced and processed were directed at the day-to-day operation of the business. In this use, managers are interactive with the computer to help them make managerial decisions. In many organizations, managers have their own computers, which use all or part of the data produced by the computer system, but the processing programs are designed for the managers.

Most companies follow this cycle step by step. In other words, the main accounting systems are put on first, followed by on-line usage of the computer to the user area, and last the decision support systems for managers are introduced. Each new step requires the involved parties to relearn their jobs. This relearning for each step goes through the following four distinct phases:

- *Phase 1—Interest and enthusiasm.* Most jobs contain tedious and boring tasks. Introducing a computer into one's work life holds the promise of eliminating those undesirable tasks and replacing them by some more interesting and challenging tasks. If all works well, life should be easier and more enjoyable for the involved party.
- *Phase 2—Chaos.* Murphy always strikes new computer systems; what can go wrong will go wrong, and at precisely the wrong moment. As the users grow disillusioned with the computer system, the self-fulfilling prophecy enters the scene. This prophecy states that the more people believe the computer is incapable of producing usable results, the less usable those results become to the users. At this point, many managers are tempted to throw the baby out with the bath water.
- *Phase 3—Control.* The method for restoring confidence in the computer system is to tightly control that system. Occasionally, this phase results in too much control, but it frequently is necessary to restore confidence in the system. Once confidence has been restored through the effective use of computer controls, the fourth and final phase can be entered.
- *Phase 4—Integration, acceptance, and usage.* This final phase puts the computer in the proper perspective. It is combining the computer, people, and control that provides usable and reliable results. Once this has occurred, the business is ready to move to a more sophisticated use of the computer.

An unfortunate, and agonizing lesson that must be learned by most businesses is that the four-phased learning process repeats on the next step, involving the more sophisticated use of the computer. As each step is introduced, the cost of learning is always a surprise, because people are optimistic and enthusiastic. It is in Phase 2 of each step that the real cost of learning occurs, and it is during this that the cost line goes up rapidly (see Fig. 1). After the control phase (Phase 3) is properly established, the failure costs drop, because people understand how to use the computer applications in their work. When the next step is introduced, those same people believe that they have already mastered the computer and thus are relatively confident that they will have few problems. Unfortunately, that's not true. The Phase 2 costs of the learning curve again increase until that step of computer technology usage is mastered. Some companies state that the more sophisticated the technology, the higher the cost of learning.

There are lessons to be learned in avoiding, anticipating, or cleaning up computer messes. These lessons will be highlighted as "cleanup rules" after the sections that discuss relevant principles. The objective of these cleanup rules is to highlight the key points covered in this book and to help identify the principles that make a computerized business environment more enjoyable.

CLEANUP RULE

Traveling an unexplored path for a new use of computer technology without the proper map, i.e., plan, is bound to lead you down a few wrong trails.

Messes don't just occur; they must be made. A wall plaque in one data processing department reads: "Don't bug me about my mistakes. Look at all the thought that went into them." We need to think for a moment about all the thought that goes into making a computer mess.

THE THEORIES OF COMPUTER MESS MAKING

After an airline crash, federal investigators examine the wreckage to pinpoint the cause. In preventing future crashes, it is important to understand the cause, so that countermeasures can be taken to prevent future crashes from the same cause. Even though these investigations may take many months and thousands of investigative hours, the cause can normally be identified. Frequently, the failure of an aircraft is due to the failure of a small component that sets off a chain reaction and eventually causes the entire airplane to malfunction.

Likewise, the cause of a computer mess can be pinpointed with sufficient investigation. Unfortunately, management frequently deals with symptoms rather than causes. For example, we may accept that a computer mess was due to an operator failure, but the real cause may be lack of adequate training or supervision or the failure to develop sufficient operating controls to ensure that the system is properly executed.

In our quest for quality data processing, we need to explore the causes of nonquality processing. The science of mess making boils down to seven theories, which are briefly described in Figure 2 and individually explained below:

1. *Rathole theory.* The rathole theory permits the continuance of a mess long after prudent management would have stopped the unfavorable situation. The rathole theory is an economic game played by project management. The theory states that everything expended on a project up to the current time should be discarded. In other words, any monies spent to date have been thrown down the rathole. The theory says that the costs and benefits of a project should be reconsidered based on current economics, and not total economics. It is this theory that causes people to invest hundreds of dollars repairing an automobile that belongs on the scrap heap because each repair is individually evaluated, so that it always appears cheaper to fix the car than to buy a new one. This theory keeps older, poorly conceived, and poorly implemented systems operational, rather than shooting them and replacing them with others that meet the true needs of the organization.

2. *GIGO theory.* The GIGO theory (garbage in, garbage out) is a transfer of blame theory. It is advocated by the data processing professional who claims no responsibility for bad input supplied by the user. The DP professional states that if the user sends the data processing department erroneous or incomplete data (garbage in) the only obligation of the data processing department is to process that bad data and send erroneous or incomplete results back to the user (garbage out).

NO.	THEORY	DESCRIPTION	ORIGINATOR
1.	Rathole	Ignore past costs and recalculate return on investment using all benefits and only future costs.	Management
2.	GIGO (Garbage in, garbage out)	DP is not responsible for accuracy or completeness, only processing whatever the user enters.	DP
3.	Torpedo	Users get shot down by poor systems that stop during processing or process incorrectly.	User
4.	Telegram	Computer systems contain a steady stream of difficult-to-understand messages describing tasks or actions that must be performed before processing can continue.	User
5.	Man on the moon	DP implies that the computer can do anything, but when the reality of processing occurs, those promises have often been compromised.	User
6.	Tough it out	Users don't take the time to learn how to use the system; they think if they just push another button things will work out.	DP
7.	Creeping commitment	Never tell anyone the full cost of doing anything; it may stop them from doing what is needed.	DP

Figure 2. The Theories of Computer Mess Making.

The data processing professional fails to recognize that most users interpret GIGO as garbage in, gospel out. Until data processing is judged on the correctness of processing, they will not become concerned with the quality of data processed and the impact of poor quality data on the business.

3. *Torpedo theory.* During wartime, a ship may sail across wide expanses of water at a leisurely pace, secure in the knowledge that no enemy vessels have been observed. On a calm day, the crew may be relaxed and enjoying the cool breezes and warm sunshine. Suddenly an explosion is heard, as an unseen torpedo launched from a submerged submarine turns calm into chaos. Users of data processing applications experience the same panic when a terminal stops processing or displays or prints some preposterously erroneous output. Users feel as helpless as the crew of the torpedoed ship. Just like the crew members, users are untrained for these unexpected events and, just like the crew, may be reluctant to get aboard the computer system again for fear that another torpedo might strike.

4. *Telegram theory.* Many used to say that nothing good ever came in a telegram. The arrival of a telegram usually meant bad news. In wartime, it frequently meant the death of a loved one. Similarly, computer messages to the user of a computer system are frequently the carriers of bad news. "Invalid—try again" says the computer when it doesn't like your password. Other messages, such as "incorrect input" or "invalid command" may only give you a clue as to what must be done to overcome a processing obstacle. Some archaic systems (in concept, not necessarily in date of origin) provide only a code that must be looked up in a manual to determine what went wrong. Too frequently, these messages are written by people who speak only "computerese" instead of everyday English.

5. *Man-on-the-moon theory.* In the early 1960s, President Kennedy announced that the United States would place a man on the moon before the end of the decade. The money process then cranked up to fuel the massive effort designed to fulfill the president's prediction. What we learned was that nothing technical is impossible if we assign enough people

and money to the task. This concept has been embraced by the data processing professional who promises to do anything with the computer, providing of course that the organization can pay for it. Unfortunately, the true costs may never be stated. If the organization's moneymaking machines fail to disgorge what is needed, the implemented system will be a compromise on the data processing promises. These compromised systems, which are the rule rather than the exception, frequently end up as a disappointment in the eyes of the user. The naive frequently believe that the computer is magic and can in fact perform all the wonderful things that are promised.

6. *Tough-it-out theory.* Data processing applications are highly structured and comprise many thousands of instructions. As is true of any technically complex subject or machine, it takes time to learn the intricacies of processing on a computer. Though the manual may say "read the instructions before using this system," many users will feel it unnecessary. Many users have minimal data processing skills, and, as we all know, a little knowledge is a dangerous thing. Many people are button pushers rather than instruction readers. They feel that it is easier to start working and using the system, rather than to spend the needed time and effort learning how to use it right. It may be a tribute to an individual's courage to keep trying in the face of continual rejection, but the cost to the business from these hardheaded approaches to computer processing may be astronomical.

7. *Creeping-commitment theory.* The creeping-commitment theory says that it is unwise to tell management the true cost of any task, because if managers don't understand the task or the need for it they may reject a valid idea based on cost alone. For example, if a young couple really knew the cost of raising a child they might never have children. Nonetheless, by eating those costs little by little over the years, and never, never adding them up, they find the costs bearable and continue to have children. If the costs associated with large data processing projects are spoon-fed to management, many events occur that would never have been permitted to happen if their real cost per benefit had been known in advance. Too

frequently, data processing is permitted to creep from a small computer to a huge computer on the easy-payment plan. It is the same easy-payment plan that has led many businesses down the road of bankruptcy.

Much work remains to be done in uncovering and clarifying the computer mess theories. Those above are representative of what permits a mess to occur. Understanding the theories should provide management with the insight to prevent a computer mess, just as the airplane crash investigator can prevent future crashes by identifying the cause of each crash. For example, if management knows that the data processing department upgrades its computer installation using the creeping commitment theory, management can be more alert and challenging of each bite-sized increase.

Sometimes it is hard to diagnose the cause of the illness until the symptoms have been identified. Knowing the symptoms of a disease is an essential ingredient in diagnosing the cause of a problem. For example, a doctor will always take a patient's temperature, blood pressure, weight, etc., because it is a combination of symptoms that leads the doctor to the cause of the illness. Let us explore for a while the symptoms of a computer mess.

CLEANUP RULE

The computer mess can be identified by the symptoms it exhibits, but management must keep in mind that a computer mess can never be cured by treating the symptoms.

SYMPTOMS OF A COMPUTER MESS

Take your car to an automobile mechanic for repair, and the first thing you will be asked is "what's wrong?" Probably you don't know what's wrong with the automobile, but you do know that there are symptoms of a problem. For example, the car may not start or the engine may be knocking or have overheated. However, the description of those symptoms is all the help the mechanic needs to begin to fix the automobile. The more precise the owner is in expressing the symptoms, the quicker the mechanic can pinpoint the problem and solve it.

NO.	SYMPTOM	DESCRIPTION	WHEN MOST LIKELY TO OCCUR
1.	Over budget	Project spends or needs more money than allocated.	At implementation time
2.	Behind schedule	Project will not be completed when needed.	At implementation time
3.	EDP staff on overtime	EDP staff works more than normal working hours.	Any time
4.	Unhappy user	User does not like the results produced by the system.	After implementation
5.	High EDP turnover	DP employees terminate the company at a 10% or greater annual rate.	With employees in 1–5-year range
6.	Out-of-balance condition	The computer-produced totals do not agree with the manually maintained totals.	At end of accounting period
7.	Excessive reruns	Computer rerun costs exceed 5% of total production operation costs.	After system changes
8.	Extensive manual adjustments	Manual adjustments exceed 1% of dollar value or number of transactions processed.	At end of accounting period
9.	Finger pointing	Blame for problems is not agreed to by involved parties.	After problems occur
10.	Numerous technological upgrades	Changes to hardware and operating software exceed six changes per year.	Before problems occur

Figure 3. Computer mess symptoms.

Management and users need to understand the symptoms of a computer mess. The cause may be attributable to some of the theories we previously discussed, but until the symptoms can be properly identified it may be difficult to fix the problem.

The most commonly exhibited symptoms of a computer mess are briefly described in Figure 3 and explained below:

- *Over budget.* Data processing projects and products should be budgeted. If the department is unable to meet those budgets, it can mean that either the budget is wrong or the project is in trouble. System development methodologies are such that it is difficult to predict the actual percentage of completion, but it is not hard to state the actual cost expenditure up to a particular time. It is not uncommon for data processing budgets to be missed by factors of 2, 3, or even 4. Therefore, a budgetary warning flag warrants managerial investigation.
- *Behind schedule.* Budgeting and scheduling symptoms are similar, but may represent different causes. For example, budgeting is a positive indication of effort, but scheduling is not. Behind schedule may be attributable to other problems in the data processing department that are causing resources to be pulled from a needed project to fight other fires in the data processing area. Regular status reports from data processing to management are essential for proper monitoring of the function.
- *EDP staff on overtime.* Well-managed data processing functions should not have to work overtime on a regular basis. Although any group can get caught in an occasional bind or work crunch, extended periods of overtime normally represent a poorly managed function. Introducing good management principles into data processing frequently eliminates overtime in a department where overtime was the rule rather than the exception.
- *Unhappy user.* Data processing tends to be the scapegoat in many organizations for a variety of problems. Nevertheless, when there is smoke there may be fire. A steady barrage of even trivial complaints from users about the functioning of the data processing department should be cause for alarm in the managerial suite. These grumblings, unless quickly addressed, can turn to the roar of users being sucked into the quicksand of inadequate computer processing.

- *High EDP turnover.* It is not an old wive's tale that rats leave a sinking ship. Nobody likes to play on a losing team, and frequently the players can foretell the outcome of the game long before the front office recognizes there is no chance of winning. When turnover is high, disregard the reason that people give for leaving, because most will say it is more money and opportunity, but the real reason is that they don't want to be associated with a computer disaster. It doesn't look good on one's résumé to state that the reason for leaving the previous employer was that they shipped the computer out and replaced it with pencil and paper.
- *Out-of-balance condition.* Computers don't make mistakes, people do. When computer systems cannot be readily reconciled to manually maintained control totals, the stench of a real mess is brewing. On-line computer systems may not have manual evidence to back up transaction processing, so that out-of-balance conditions may mean erroneous record keeping and loss of assets to the business. Even small out-of-balance conditions should incite management to quick action.
- *Excessive reruns.* A rerun in a computer is like an erasure on a manually maintained record. If the answer was wrong, the preparer erases the answer and recalculates it. If the computer fails to produce the proper results, the system is rerun. Some reruns can be expected, just as some manual errors can be expected, but this problem symptom, like body temperature, becomes more serious as it increases.
- *Finger pointing.* Bickering among the various operating departments is par for the course. All the same, when one group begins to blame another for operating deficiencies, the rivalry warrants investigation. A house divided cannot stand. When a user department has exhausted its corrective options, or when the data processing department senses that a user is out to sabotage the function, fingers begin to point to build the case for pinpointing blame when the disaster occurs. The real loser may be corporate profitability.
- *Numerous technological upgrades.* Poorly constructed and operated computer systems consume huge amounts of operational resources. The misuse of the computer can be like a leech sucking processing capacity faster than the organization

can replenish it. A continual barrage of requests to add more computer memory, disk capacity, processing speed, additional input/output devices, more terminals, etc., indicate a system mess that is inappropriately being solved by overpowering it with processing capacity.

Study these symptoms carefully, and be on the lookout for them. Remember though that they are symptoms and not causes of the problem. Data processing is a triangle involving senior management, data processing, and users. The cause can be located in any corner of the triangle. Don't confuse the symptom with the cause until adequate investigation has been undertaken. Equally important, don't ignore the symptoms, because the cost of ignoring them may far exceed the cost of immediate corrective action.

CLEANUP RULE
The cost of ignoring computer problems can be disastrous. The expression "you can pay me now, or you can pay me later" is as applicable to a computer problem as it is to an automotive transmission problem.

THE REAL CAUSES OF A COMPUTER MESS

The cause of a computer mess should not be confused with a cure for the mess. To many people, the cure is more painful than the illness. For example, some people may live with crooked teeth: they know the cause is having too many teeth, but they do not want to accept the cure of having those teeth pulled.

Twenty-five-plus years of data processing experience has taught us how to do data processing right. However, one need only observe the frequency and intensity of automobile accidents to understand that knowing how to do it right and doing it right are two entirely different aspects.

In the next few sentences we can describe the causes of most computer messes, but we will require the rest of the book and a significant amount of your time, effort, and patience to remedy the situation. Let's quickly unveil the five causes of most computer messes:

1. Inadequate computer planning — The primary cause of most computer failures is the insufficient resources and effort allocated to planning. Computers are often purchased as impulse items, rather than to satisfy an information processing need. Systems are developed without planning the manual interfaces. Staffing is based on budgetary constraints, rather than on the skills and staff needed to effectively implement computer applications. Planning is a managerial function frequently ignored by technicians or done to satisfy managerial whim, not to establish a blueprint to be followed in automating the organization.

2. Inability to integrate the computer into the organizational structure — The primary objective of the computer is to assist the information processing requirements of the organization. Data may be the major resource of every organization. It is not owned by the data processing department or the individual users who create and use the data. Until data is managed as an organizational resource, it will not receive the appropriate managerial attention, and thus it will be relegated to a level where its use may be unplanned and poorly managed. It is truly unfortunate that data is not capitalized, so that it can be managed like other capital assets of an organization. Management might let data deteriorate, but it would never consider letting the physical plant deteriorate.

3. Failure to develop the necessary data processing skills — Management has the responsibility to ensure that its staff is adequately skilled. This involves hiring the right people, providing them with any additional training necessary to develop or improve skills, and evaluating performance to ensure that the staff is performing its job adequately. Because of the technical nature of data processing, management may feel insecure in assessing the needed skills, forcing them to rely on third parties for hiring, and to equate previous experience with competence. Users also require some technical training. The system works when the chief executive officer of the organization attends computer courses, becomes conversant with the language of computers, and takes a personal interest in the success of automation in the organization.

4. Inability to implement user requirements correctly — The development of requirements does not appear to be a productive function to technicians. System design, programming, and testing are work for which you can see the results. Too many systems are built before the architecture of the system has finished the blueprint. Too many users agree to a system before they know exactly what they are getting. Implementing what others say they want or agree is what they want is worthless if it doesn't do the needed job.

5. Failure to provide adequate computer controls — In an ideal environment, in which everything works perfectly, controls are unnecessary. Unfortunately, computer systems are rarely ideal and require control. As previously discussed, manual controls may not be effective in an automated system. The controls designed for an automated system must complement the characteristics of the computer. This means a restructuring of controls by someone who understands both the business and the computer.

These causes of computer problems can be restated into the five following golden rules of computer processing:

- Golden Rule 1 — Develop both long-range and short-range computer plans, and then follow those plans.
- Golden Rule 2 — Appoint a senior officer responsible for data and integrating the use of the computer into the organization.
- Golden Rule 3 — Hire the best technical brains available, continue to develop their skills, and evaluate their ability to perform their jobs properly. If the individuals cannot master the needed skills, replace them.
- Golden Rule 4 — Don't acquire or implement a computerized business application until the requirements have been thoroughly defined and agreed to by all parties.
- Golden Rule 5 — Devise and maintain a system of computer controls adequate to ensure the accurate, complete, authorized, and timely processing of data.

ROAD MAP THROUGH THE BOOK

This book is designed for the three parties who have been directly or indirectly involved in making the mess and now have responsibility for cleaning up the mess:

- Senior management — The senior officers of the corporation, including the officer to whom the data processing manager reports.
- Data processing management — The individuals responsible for the operation of the data processing function.
- User management — Those operational areas of the company that provide data to and receive results from computerized applications.

Those sections of the book that are of specific interest to each of the three audiences are designated in Figure 4. This shows the audience for which the chapter was primarily written and the audience that can benefit from the insight in the chapter on solving a specific computer problem (designated as secondary audience).

Senior management is responsible for the quality of data of the organization, and thus any problems that impair the quality or time-liness of data become a senior management problem. The book is designed to help senior management identify problems before they become serious and then to address those problems, such as organizational structure and staffing, which are managerial responsibilities. The success of many user departments depends upon the correctness and timeliness of processing. This book provides sufficient information to give users an early warning of potentially serious data processing problems and then provides them solutions and approaches to help them get out of trouble before a major disaster occurs. Data processing is a technical function, frequently run by technicians. Unfortunately, many of the more serious computer problems are not technical problems but, rather, people and organizational problems. The book is designed to help the data processing professional fit computerized applications into the organizational structure in a manner that minimizes problems by identifying the type of problems that must be addressed in computer design, implementation, and operation.

CHAPTERS		AUDIENCE		
NO.	TITLE	SENIOR MANAGEMENT	USERS	EDP
1.	How Does a Computer Mess Originate	P	P	P
2.	Diagnosing the Problem	S	S	P
3.	Solving an Organizational Dispute	P	S	S
4.	Solving a Vendor Problem	S		P
5.	Solving a Changing Business Requirement Need		P	S
6.	Solving a Misuse of the System Problem		P	S
7.	Solving a Programming Problem	S		P
8.	Solving a Technical Staffing Problem	P		S
9.	Solving an Unusable Output Problem		P	S
10.	Solving a Disaster Situation	S		P
11.	Solving a Space Management Problem	S		P
12.	Solving a Computer Capacity Problem	S		P
13.	Avoiding the Recurrence of a Computer Mess	P	S	S

P = Primary audience
S = Secondary audience

Figure 4. Road map through the book.

The book is divided into the following three parts:

- *Part 1 — So Now You Are in Trouble.* Up to this point, the book has described the problem. The objective of this chapter is to explain what can go wrong and why it goes wrong. Chapter 2 is a diagnostic process to help the readers identify computer problems in their organizations, and then to point the readers to the specific chapter in the book that covers the solution to that problem.
- *Part 2 — How to Get Your Computer Back on Track.* The objective of this part of the book is to provide readily implementable solutions to the more common computer system problems. The chapters in this part explain how to implement the five golden rules of computer processing. The rule on integrating the computer into the organizational structure is addressed in Chapters 3 and 4. Chapter 3 explains how to solve an organizational dispute, and Chapter 4 discusses how to make the best use of vendors and how to resolve vendor problems.

    The golden rule of ensuring that the real needs of the user are handled by the automated application are discussed in Chapters 5 and 6. Chapter 5 explains how to ensure that the right requirements get into the application system and how those systems can be kept current with the changing business needs. Chapter 6 addresses training and the problems associated with the misuse of computer systems.

    The golden rule on hiring and developing the appropriate skills in the developers and users of applications is explained in Chapters 7 and 8. Chapter 7 explores programming problems and explains how to resolve programming defects. Chapter 8 explores the problems in staffing, training, communicating, and integrating the data processing technician into the mission of the business.

    The golden rule on developing and operating computer controls is addressed in Chapters 9 and 10. Chapter 9 handles the dilemma of what to do when outputs are incorrect or incomplete. Chapter 10 explains how to avoid a disaster, as well as what to do when one occurs.

    The golden rule on planning from a computer resource perspective is covered in Chapters 11 and 12. Chapter 11 deals with the problem of too much data and too little space. Chapter 12 provides some escape mechanisms for the lack of computer capacity, as well as information about how to develop plans to avoid running out of capacity.

- *Part 3 — Avoiding Problems in the Future.* Chapter 13 explains what you need to do to stop living on a hand-to-mouth basis in the computer area. With the current intensity of competition and the difficult economic times, management doesn't need a computer problem. This chapter provides a plan of action for management to implement to avoid the recurrence of the type of problems it may have experienced in the past.

CLEANUP RULE

When a computer mess occurs, senior management must bite the bullet, roll up its sleeves, and jump into the data processing function. The odds are that if the data processing department got into a serious mess, it will not be able to get out of it without senior management assistance.

2
DIAGNOSING THE PROBLEM

A computerized business environment is like a house of cards. When the first one falls, the rest may come tumbling down shortly thereafter. The best method to avoid the collapse of a business's information processing system is to diagnose the weak link early and take corrective action before the crash occurs.

The key to success in many organizations is the ability to diagnose problems and recommend solutions. Because the computer is one of the most valuable tools of the organization, and at the same time may be its greatest headache, it promises a bonanza of opportunities for the problem solver. Frequently, diagnosing the problem is more difficult than developing the solution.

The diagnostician of computer problems need not be a technician. This is because most computer problems are business problems, not technical problems. Data processing technicians are very effective in solving technical problems, but may not be aware of or able to solve business problems.

The diagnostic approach presented in this chapter is that of a manager and a consultant. It is designed to assist in the identification of the problem. Once the problem has been identified, an investigation can be undertaken and a solution developed. The approach presented in this chapter points to the later chapters in the book that contain the solutions to the problems.

THE REALM OF THE HIGH PRIESTS AND PRIESTESSES

Data processing is frequently referred to as a black art. The computer itself has been called the black box. Obviously, those having mystical powers over the black box must be the high priests and priestesses of the black art of computer sciences.

The rites of this art include:

- A language called computerese, comprising groups of letters such as COBOL, JCL, POWER, and BASIC, which stand for either a combination of words or a secret symbol or password.
- Highly sophisticated codes called EBCDIC and HEXADECIMAL, into which data is translated from easy-to-read English.
- Speed, one of the goddesses of this priesthood, moves data so fast that new terminology must be coined, such as *nanosecond,* to express the speed of processing.
- Ritual and methodology; these are important to this priesthood. Things must be done by the numbers, which creates the need for a whole new terminology to express the sequence in which events occur, such as systems development life cycle, structured design, and structured programming.

Enter now into the scene mortal men and women. Their lives are changed by this black art, and they become obedient to the rules and schedules provided by the high priests and priestesses. If all goes well, we can be happy to leave the priesthood in its sealed quarters. When problems occur, however, and our jobs and responsibilities are affected, we, the mortals, must take action.

The question that must be answered is: Can the nontechnician diagnose problems associated with that technology?   The answer to that question may be found as you ponder the following questions:

- If you encountered a problem with your automobile, could you isolate whether that problem was associated with the steering mechanism, the tires, the engine, or the cooling system?
- If your television failed to work, could you diagnose the problem as loss of power to the house, failure to plug the television set into the wall socket, or a problem inside the television set?
- If your lawnmower failed to start, could you diagnose the problem as lack of gasoline, failure to use the choke, or an engine problem?

The above diagnoses can be made by someone with minimal familiarity with the technical aspects of the product being evaluated. Likewise, the user and the manager can diagnose and determine the cause of a lot of computer system problems.   The system comprises the computer, data, programs, data processing professional, input transactions, and a varitey of other components that must all work together to produce accurate, complete, and timely results. One should not overestimate the internal technical functioning of the computer as an impediment to pinpointing computer problems.

CLEANUP RULE

To err is human, to blame it on the other guy is even more human.

HOW TO DIAGNOSE A COMPUTER PROBLEM

How frequently have you been involved in an unfavorable situation that appeared uncorrectable and thought "If I only knew what the problem was, I could solve it." We run into these situations when someone appears mad at us and we do not know why, or we encounter some periodic problem with our automobile that never happens when the mechanic is looking at it. Knowing what is wrong is the primary prerequisite to the solution.

Computer problems tend to intimidate us, as do other high-technological problems. For example, if the picture on our television set lost its color, we might feel lost. Yet, let's look at what we would know about the situation:

1. A color set that is supposed to show a color picture fails to display the picture in color.
2. The set worked right at one time and no longer works.
3. The problem occurred abruptly.
4. The change of condition is permanent; in other words, it no longer displays a color picture at any time.
5. All other operating characteristics appear normal.
6. The user (that's you) is dissatisfied with the performance of the set.
7. The set is or is not under a guarantee period.

This list could be extended, but the items are representative of those defining a television problem. Until the problem can be expressed in those types of terms to the repair person, that individual may not be able to fix the set. We know, for example, that periodic problems are more difficult to correct than consistent problems. We also know that the more clearly we can describe the problem, the easier fixing the problem becomes. We also know that the more we know about the problem, the more difficult it is for the technician to snow us technically about the problem, the solution, the timing of the solution, and the cost of the solution.

A matrix for diagnosing and solving the problem (see Figure 5) is provided to help nontechnicians address technical computer problems. This matrix presents an orderly method for analyzing an unfavorable computer event. All that the user of the matrix must know is that that individual has some concern about the computer area. For example, a needed report may be late, an amount on a computer report may be wrong, or two subordinates may be bickering over the correct solution to a stated computer need.

The matrix provides the following five diagnostic aids:

- Concern questions — A series of questions are provided for the user to ask about each computer concern. The user of the matrix picks the question or questions that will challenge the facts surrounding the concern.
- Challenging the answer to the concern question — The information provided in answer to the question should be challenged as to whether or not the answer represents the proper way to do the job. To a large degree, challenging the answer will identify the cause of the problem. It is the cause that represents the real problem and not the symptoms that usually raise the concern.
- Most likely problem — The matrix provides the most probable problem for each of the areas challenged by a question.
- Good business practice violated — If the problem is that suggested as the most likely problem, then the good business practice that has been violated is identified. It is the correction of the violation of the good business practice that will solve the problem.
- Problem solution — The most probable solutions are then listed to solve the problem. The solution selected is designed to reinstate the good business practice, which in most instances will eliminate the cause of the problem.

ABOUT EACH CONCERN ASK THE QUESTION:	CHALLENGE THE ANSWER;	IF A PROBLEM THE MOST LIKELY PROBLEM IS THAT THE TASK IS:	THE GOOD BUSINESS PRACTICE THAT HAS BEEN VIOLATED IS:	THE SOLUTION TO THE PROBLEM TASK IS TO:
WHAT is done?	WHY THAT?	NONESSENTIAL, REDUNDANT	PRODUCTIVITY, NEED	ELIMINATE
WHERE is it done?	WHY THERE?	INCONVENIENT LOCATION	SMOOTH FLOW	REARRANGE
WHEN is it done?	WHY THEN?	POOR SEQUENCE	SMOOTH FLOW	REARRANGE
WHO does it?	WHY HIM?	FRAGMENTED, IMPROPER SKILLS	PRODUCTIVITY, FLOW	CHANGE, COMBINE
HOW is it done?	WHY THAT WAY?	COMPLICATED, COSTLY	SIMPLICITY	IMPROVE
WHY is it done?	WHY PERMITTED?	NONCOM-PLIANCE, INEFFECTIVE	COMPLIANCE	COMPLY, REVISE

Figure 5. Matrix for diagnosing and solving a problem.

Let's consider for a minute how the matrix might work with the problem of a late computer report. The most obvious question to ask about the concern is: "When is it done?" Management would ask that question of the data processing people and the users involved. When the answer is provided, it would be challenged by the question: "Why then?" If the timing sounds reasonable, then management would go on to another question; however, if the timing is not reasonable and the "why then" question is not properly answered, then the most likely problem that has caused the report to be late is a poor sequencing of events. This occurs because the good business practice of "smooth flow" has been violated. The cause might be in the system itself, the preparation or delivery of input data, or the decollating and distribution of output reports. The obvious solution to such a problem is to rearrange the sequence in which the events are performed.

Most computer problems can be diagnosed using the Figure 5 matrix. Obviously, a single-word solution is too simplistic, and additional study must be done to develop an effective implementation of that solution. This process will be addressed at the end of the chapter. The objective of this matrix is to identify the cause of the problem and a managerial solution objective. For example, if management can state that it wants tasks rearranged so that reports will be delivered by a specific time or date, that is normally sufficient direction to the data processing people to develop and implement a solution to the problem. The less specific management is in describing a problem and explaining its desired objectives, however, the less likely it is to get the desired solution.

CLEANUP RULE

Praise improves the mood of the developer, but criticism improves the quality of the product.

MANAGERIAL COMPUTER DIAGNOSTIC TOOLS

The solution matrix can be supplemented by other diagnostic tools. In some instances, experience expressed in the form of a solution matrix quickly pinpoints the problem. In other instances, it's necessary to raise the hood of the car and probe deeper to find the true cause of the problem. The effective solution to some computer messes requires more sophisticated diagnostic tools.

A diagnostic tool is a device, or aid, to help management in the diagnostic process. An automotive mechanic or an engineer will use mechanical devices to test such things as the compression, the proper aiming of the headlights, and the voltage at a specific point in the engine. Unfortunately, there are no equivalent managerial tools to tie to the computer system to evaluate the performance. The technician has some of these tools, but, like the voltage meter, they are tools designed for the technician, not the manager.

The three computer mess diagnostic tools that can be effectively used by management are:

1. Smell test — An awareness test as to whether or not the computer is being properly utilized.
2. Analytical test — A mathematical evaluation to show in numerical format the good news or bad news of the data processing function.
3. Probing test — Structured managerial questioning designed to uncover flaws in proposed or implemented data processing applications.

These are the basic diagnostic tools used by management in any problem situation. The applicability and use of those tools in diagnosing a computer mess will be individually discussed.

The Smell Test

Management has been using the smell test for hundreds of years. Some state that the smell test is the application of experience to a business situation. In many instances, the manager has lived through this type of situation before, so that, once the problem begins to reappear, recognizing those symptoms is all that is needed to "smell" a forthcoming problem. For example, let us assume that after weeks of corporate bickering about specifications and responsibilities an application system was late in being installed. If this cycle repeated, and then with the new application management again perceived this bickering, it could with a high probability predict that that application would be late in being installed. This is the smell test.

The only difference between the smell test in data processing and any other area of the business is the odor the manager is smelling for. The more familiar with data processing the manager becomes, the easier it will be to identify the odor of a computer mess.

Some of the more common computer smell tests are briefly described in Figure 6 and described in more detail below (note that Figure 6 shows the chapter reference where the solution to the identified problem is discussed):

- *Smell test 1 — Users and DP personnel are preparing alibi files.* An alibi file is the documentation needed to substantiate one's innocence as either culprit or contributing factor in a computer mess. Astute employees are quick to identify a potential disaster. The survivors quickly dissociate themselves from the project or, if they can't dissociate themselves, go on record in foretelling the doom and identifying the guilty parties. At a meeting of a computer project that later turned out to be a disaster, one of the early proponents and participants never again returned to a meeting or had his name associated with any project document. It has been said that many current data processing managers were successful in getting off every project they were assigned to prior to that project being placed into production.

  Alibi file symptoms include:

  — Letters for the record raising concern
  — Minority opinions attached to meeting minutes
  — Clear and prominent identification of who proposed what
  — Confirmation letters to management reconfirming that what it said it wants is what it really wants

- *Smell test 2 — A high frequency of meetings and visits from vendors.* Some state that there is quiet before the storm, while others recognize the quiet activities leading up to the storm. In a computer mess, many of these quiet activities are an attempt to negotiate a workable system prior to implementation. Other indications are visits from third parties, particularly vendors who have a vested interest in the solution, to help resolve problems.

NO.	SMELL TEST	EVALUATION OF TEST	SEE CHAPTER
1.	Users and DP personnel are preparing alibi files	If the parties involved in DP are building their case to assign responsibility for a failure, a failure may not be far off.	3
2.	A high frequency of meetings and visits from vendors	The less agreement between parties, the more the reasons to meet to resolve differences. Also, the presence of third parties (e.g., vendor or consultants), the higher the probability of problems.	3, 4, 8
3.	Late reports	You can deliver junk. A long time to prepare an acceptable report usually means the mess has occurred.	9, 10, 11, 12
4.	Increases in overtime hours worked (paid or unpaid)	If they don't work they must be fixed. If they can't be fixed in normal working hours, it usually means abnormal problems.	5, 6, 7

Figure 6. Smelling a computer mess.

These activities are desirable activities. Management should not discourage the meetings, but should recognize that they may foretell problems. In a well-constructed computer system, problems are resolved prior to design and implementation. In problem systems, difficulties are often glossed over in requirements (a period of wild excitement), but smolder until implementation, at which point decisions can no longer be delayed.

The characteristics of a troubled system development project or an implemented project are:

— A reworking of requirements
— A rerun of project outputs
— Use of vendors as arbiters
— Use of vendors to make presentations to users
— Delaying making decisions until a following meeting
— Involving operating management in decision making that should be resolved at the staff level

• *Smell test 3 — Late reports.* The inability to meet deadlines previously agreed to smells of problems. The reasons may sound logical, such as hardware problems, reworking of requirements, developing newer low-cost solutions, etc., but many of these excuses are merely symptoms of some underlying serious systems problems.

Late reports cover a variety of data processing outputs. In the developmental stage, this can mean system design, report mockups, etc. For operational systems it can be that the system is running late, that it is rerun, or that specific reports, including inputs, cannot be put in a deliverable format or their integrity verified at the scheduled delivery time.

The attributes to smell for regarding late reports include:

— Reports delivered and then retrieved for reworking
— Delays for which no expected delivery time can be stated
— Partial delivery on computer system output reports
— Output report problems associated with incorrect input preparation by the user

• *Smell test 4 — Increases in overtime hours worked (paid or unpaid).* Another form of increased activity associated with computer problems is extra hours worked. In many instances, these are unpaid hours that apparently are performed by dedicated employees. In many instances, the dedication is to keeping their jobs, rather than losing them. Unfortunately, many of these "dedicated" employees are only buying time until they can find another job in a company that is not fouled up.

It is not unusual for data processing to hit peak work periods requiring extra hours to complete. What management should be alert to are changes in normal work patterns. Short bursts of overtime may not be cause for concern, but long-term (over one week) changes in work patterns usually indicate that the department has buried itself in a problem that is difficult to get out of.

Some of the indicators that should raise a red warning flag regarding overtime include:

— Work on Sundays and holidays
— Changes in work patterns
— Addition of an extra operating shift without associated known changes in workload
— Data processing manager living in company quarters
— DP personnel skipping lunch, company affairs, and asking to be excused from nonessential meetings

The above smell tests are representative of areas that management should be alert to. Other types of smell tests that senior management may want to consider regarding data processing include:

• Rapid escalations in data processing budget
• Excessive user complaints
• High turnover in data processing
• Unexpected increases in equipment
• Unexpected requests to hire additional personnel

The Analytical Test

Accounting is the tool of management. Through accounting, management can develop analytical information that indicates how the organization is doing. For example, such general measures as gross profit and net profit provide an overall indication of the success of the organization; more specific analyses, such as inventory turnover, age of accounts receivables, product breakage, and product returns, help evaluate internal performance.

NO.	RELATIONSHIPS EVALUATED	EVALUATION OF TEST	SEE CHAPTER
1.	Cost of DP services in relation to total business sales	DP services in a new shop should be about 1 percent of sales, in a mature shop, 3 percent	8
2.	Trend of increases from year to year in performing DP services	If DP cost increase exceeds inflation and business growth, it may need to be subject to more control	3, 4, 8
3.	Number of versions of computer systems installed each year into production	Installing more than one new version a month is normally more change than people can assimilate	5, 7
4.	Cost to process a business transaction (point in time and trend)	The cost needed to process a business transaction on the computer should be compared to the cost of manual processing to determine the rate of change	6, 7, 11, 12
5.	Cost to maintain an application in relation to the cost to develop OR Cost to install an application in relation to the cost to acquire that application	Maintenance should not exceed 50 percent of development cost and ideally would be about 25 percent of development cost	5, 7, 8
6.	Over budget, behind schedule, or both	The situations represent poor planning and poor management of data processing resources	5, 7, 8, 9, 10
7.	DP work backlog in months to accomplish	The average backlog is three years of work and is unacceptable; a three-month backlog is reasonable and should not be exceeded	5, 7, 11, 12

Figure 7. Analytical tests to uncover a computer mess.

Most mature functions of a business provide the information needed to analyze the internal performance of that function. Data processing is a relatively new function that has not yet developed generally accepted evaluators, such as inventory turnover. Some of the indicators that have been used, such as source statements written per programmer per hour, have been poor evaluation tests.

Seven analytical tests to uncover the computer mess are listed in Figure 7. This figure lists the tests, explains how to evaluate the test results, and then points to the chapter in the book in which the problem solution is discussed. The process of gathering the information and producing the information to be evaluated is discussed below:

- *Analytical test 1 − Cost of services.* This test shows the relationship between the cost of DP services and the total business sales. The cost of DP services would include people, computer facilities, space, consultants and rental charges, and any amortization of hardware and software purchases. Business sales should be the method of describing revenue, which can be sales, budget, earned premiums, etc. The national average is about 3 percent for a mature data processing function. Note that management should attempt to get a more appropriate figure for its industry, as some businesses are more computerized than others.
- *Analytical test 2 − Cost trends.* This test shows the trend produced from test no. 1 over a period of time. The trend produced by one company's data processing function showed that if the particular percentage of increase were to continue for another fourteen years the company would be spending more on data processing services than it took in from sales. The trend of increase in a new function can be expected to exceed the annual increase in sales, but in a more mature data processing function it should be in line with sales increases unless significantly new functions are being undertaken by the data processing department.
- *Analytical test 3 − Frequency of change.* This test shows the relationship between application systems in the number of new versions being installed in the course of a year. A new version of an application system is one that has been modified or extended. People's ability to assimilate change into their work

patterns is limited. When changes come too quickly, employees cannot differentiate between what they were asked to do yesterday and what they are being asked to do today, versus how it will change again tomorrow. Normally, applications with the highest frequency of change are the problem applications. Note that management should also be concerned about applications with no changes, because the usefulness of those systems may have passed and users may have developed other means of accomplishing their information processing requirements.

- *Analytical test 4 — Cost to process a business transaction.* This test shows the relationship between the total cost to operate an application and the number of business transactions being processed by that application. For example, the business transaction may be a customer invoice. The cost to operate the application should be limited to the computer area, but include people costs involved in maintaining and operating the application, as well as computer time charges. These costs should be calculated at both a single point in time and as a trend over a period of months or years. It would be helpful if this cost could be compared with the manual cost to process a transaction prior to computerization.

- *Analytical test 5 — Maintenance cost of a computerized application.* The cost of maintaining computerized applications is normally significantly higher than that experienced in maintaining manual applications. This is because most of the changes deal with exception processing, and in a manual system these do not need to be addressed by the system, but can be addressed at the point where they occur. In a computerized application they must be handled by the system, and frequently before they occur or become serious. The cost to maintain an application is the total people and machine costs directly attributable to modifying and enhancing the application system in relationship to a fixed amount. In an in-house-developed application the cost to maintain should be compared with the cost to develop the application; in a purchased application, however, a more realistic comparison is the cost to install changes and enhancements versus the cost to acquire the application. Once this amount is known, it can be compared with the value received from making that change to indicate the type of return on investment the organization is getting from maintaining its system. Note again that problem systems tend to have more changes and thus a greater cost to maintain than well-developed application systems.

- *Analytical test 6 — Over budget, behind schedule, or both.* This test shows two relationships. First is the relationship of actual cost to budgeted cost for the development, maintenance, or operation of a computer application. Second is the actual performance date versus the scheduled performance date. The number of comparisons to be made will depend upon the number of managerial checkpoints, such as milestones or frequency of operations. Some leeway should be allowed, such as plus or minus 5 percent over or under budget, or some realistic tolerance in meeting the schedule, such as to produce a report within plus or minus two hours of the scheduled date or implement a change within plus or minus two days of the scheduled date. Management should note that those projects that are habitually behind tend to stay behind. When the first milestone is missed, management should not expect that time to be made up, because it rarely is.

- *Analytical test 7 — Measurement of data processing backlog.* The IBM Corporation has stated that the typical organization has a three-year backlog of data processing work. One of the reasons attributable to the rapid growth of personal computers in business is the attempt by users to reduce this backlog. Information is one of the most valuable resources an organization has. If it takes three years of work to provide the type of information that management desires, it is possible that the organization is at a competitive disadvantage because of the lag in needed information. This measurement requires data processing to identify and estimate the amount of time required to complete the current work backlog, and then to express it in terms of months to accomplish, based upon the current staffing and other workload commitments.

In using analytical tests, management must differentiate between symptoms of problems and causes of problems. The number produced by the analytical test is a symptom, not a cause. For example, a high number of versions of an application system is a symptom of a problem.   In banking, the cause may be extensive changes by the comptroller of the currency, or it may be attributable to the fact that the system was poorly designed and the user is trying to re-structure it into something useful.   Once the test has been con-ducted, the result must be analyzed to determine the cause of the problem.   These, like the smell test, are designed more to help management identify the problem than to uncover the cause and develop a solution.

CLEANUP RULE
Whatever can go wrong will go wrong, and at precisely the wrong time.

Problem Diagnostic Decision Table

The most common management problem identification technique is probing.   Probing is an investigative technique that uses questioning as the vehicle for gathering information.   The more structured the questioning, the likelier that it will produce meaningful results — in other words, identify the problem.

Management primarily uses probing after it has been presented a proposal.   The objectives of the probing are to clarify points in the proposal and to identify items that may have been inadequately dis-cussed or disclosed.

Probing when the area to probe has not been identified, such as through a presentation to management, is more difficult to execute. The difference is that the area of probing is less defined to both the prober and those being probed.

Probing is most successful in the data processing environment when a problem is suspected.   The probing test works well in con-junction with the smell test and analytical test.   As these tests iden-tify an area of concern, management can use the probing test to ex-plore that area.

A diagnostic decision table is presented in Figure 8 to help man-agement with this computer mess probing.   A decision table is a structured method of presenting questions.   The objective of the

NO.	ITEM	IF YES GO TO	IF NO GO TO	ACTION
1.	Has operation of the computer system terminated?	10	2	
2.	Have the outputs of the computer system been evaluated and determined to be inaccurate or incomplete?	20	3	
3.	Has the performance of the computer center degraded to a level of concern?	30	4	
4.	Does the user need information not included on the computer outputs?	40	5	
5.	Has data provided by the user to the computer center been lost?	50	6	
6.	Are you dissatisfied with the performance of the EDP function?	60	STOP No further action required	
10.	Is the problem due to a hardware malfunction?	ACTION	11	Read Chapter 4
11.	Is the problem due to a failure in the software system provided by a software vendor?	ACTION	12	Read Chapter 4
12.	Is the problem due to a failure in a system developed in-house?	ACTION	13	Read Chapter 7
13.	Is the problem due to incorrectly entered input to the system?	ACTION	14	Read Chapter 6
14.	Is the problem due to incorrect operation of the computer, associated terminals, or both?	ACTION	15	Read Chapter 8
15.	Is the problem due to a natural or man-made disaster?	ACTION	Hire a consultant to help diagnose the problem	Read Chapter 10
20.	Are parts of the physical output missing (e.g., pages missing from a report)?	ACTION	21	Read Chapter 9
21.	Are individual transactions processed incorrectly?	ACTION	22	Read Chapter 7
22.	Are transactions that have not been entered into the computer system missing from the processed data?	ACTION	23	Read Chapter 9

Figure 8. Problem diagnostic decision table (cont.)

NO.	ITEM	IF YES GO TO	IF NO GO TO	ACTION
23.	Do unexpected transactions appear in output reports?	ACTION	24	Read Chapter 9
24.	Are the detailed records in the computer files out of balance with the computer-maintained control totals?	ACTION	25	Read Chapter 9
25.	Is the computer-produced control total out of balance with the manually maintain control total?	ACTION	Hire a consultant to help diagnose the problem	Read Chapter 7
30.	Has poorly functioning hardware caused the degradation of computer service?	ACTION	31	Read Chapter 4
31.	Have operator problems caused extensive system reruns?	ACTION	32	Read Chapter 8
32.	Is processing slowed due to processing loads exceeding computer capacity?	ACTION	33	Read Chapter 12
33.	Is processing slowed due to data file size exceeding reasonable load levels?	ACTION	34	Read Chapter 11
34.	Is processing slowed due to excessive data entry errors?	ACTION	35	Read Chapter 6
35.	Has poorly functioning vendor-supplied operating software caused the degradation of computer service?	ACTION	36	Read Chapter 4
36.	Are processing delays attributable to the inability to collect data from multiple departments on a timely basis?	ACTION	37	Read Chapter 3
37.	Are inefficient application systems attributable to poor programming practices?	ACTION	Hire a consultant to help diagnose the problem	Read Chapter 7
40.	Was the needed information specified in the system requirements?	ACTION	41	Read Chapter 7
41.	Has the needed information been requested, but not yet implemented?	ACTION	42	Read Chapter 5
42.	Can the needed information be obtained from the system but the user doesn't know how to get it?	ACTION	43	Read Chapter 6

Figure 8. Problem diagnostic decision table (cont.)

NO.	ITEM	IF YES GO TO	IF NO GO TO	ACTION
43.	Is the needed information missing because the "owner" of the application hasn't requested it?	ACTION	44	Read Chapter 3
44.	Has a vendor of software refused to supply a needed capability?	ACTION	Hire a consultant to help diagnose the problem	Read Chapter 4
50.	Has data been lost because users were not involved in disaster recovery plans?	ACTION	51	Read Chapter 3
51.	Was needed data lost because it was not saved long enough?	ACTION	52	Read Chapter 10
52.	Was data lost due to application system failures?	ACTION	53	Read Chapter 7
53.	Was data lost due to hardware failures?	ACTION	54	Read Chapter 4
54.	Could the lost data be reconstructed?	ACTION	55	Read Chapter 10
55.	Has a disaster plan been developed and tested?	ACTION	Hire a consultant to help diagnose the problem	Read Chapter 10
60.	Is cooperation between DP and users unsatisfactory?	ACTION	61	Read Chapter 3
61.	Is the cost-effectiveness of data processing unsatisfactory?	ACTION	62	Read Chapter 8
62.	Are you dissatisfied with the plans and programs of the data processing department?	ACTION	63	Read Chapter 8
63.	Are you dissatisfied with vendor products, service, or both?	ACTION	64	Read Chapter 4
64.	Are you dissatisfied with the amount of time required to install a system change?	ACTION	65	Read Chapter 5
65.	Does the DP function seem unable to acquire additional hardware in a reasonable time?	ACTION	66	Read Chapter 12
66.	Are you dissatisfied with all the complaints stated about data processing service?	ACTION	Hire a consultant to help diagnose the problem	Read Chapter 3

Figure 8. Problem diagnostic decision table (cont.)

decision table is to lead the user through the series of questions to a specific action to perform.

Decision tables are significantly different from checklists. Checklists contain a series of items that pertain to a particular area. The user of the checklist covers all the items in an effort to ensure the propriety or problems associated with a specific area. The decision table, however, includes more questions than are needed to address a specific problem. In a decision table the answer to one question leads the user to the next question to be asked, and so on, until finally the question itself indicates the action that needs to be performed.

The Computer Problem Diagnostic Decision Table (Figure 8) is used as follows:

1. Begin with item (question) no. 1.
2. If the answer to that question is yes, the user jumps to the question number indicated in the yes column.
3. If the answer to an item is no, the user jumps to the question number indicated in the no column.
4. If the information in the yes or no column is the word ACTION, then the reader should perform the action indicated in the action column. In all instances, this will direct the reader to the appropriate chapter that addresses the problem raised in the question.
5. If the information in the book cannot help the user, in other words, if a generalized action cannot be described for the problem, then the no column will indicate an alternative process to undertake, such as hire a consultant.

The use of the diagnostic decision table is twofold. First, it will help diagnose the problem. This will happen when the yes answer indicates that an action is to be taken. Second, the decision table points the reader to the chapter where the specific problem will be addressed. The problem relates to the item that caused the action to occur.

COMPUTER MESS PROBLEM SOLVING

Once the cause of the problem has been identified, management is ready to initiate action to solve that problem. Unfortunately, data processing encompasses many segments of the organization, making it difficult to dictate workable solutions. One must remember that if the solution was easy, the problem may not have existed.

A workable approach to solving data processing problems is presented in Figure 9. This eight-step process is designed to produce a workable and acceptable plan of action to overcome a problem. It takes into account the magic of technology and the impact of that technology on people. It does what the industrial psychologist says must be done: it involves people in solving their own problems.

The remainder of the book is directed at offering solutions. Unfortunately, knowing the solution does not necessarily correct a wrong. For example, people know that smoking causes cancer, and the absence of seat belts increases the probability of being injured in an automobile accident. Knowing this information does not necessarily stop people from smoking or cause them to buckle their seat belts.

Listed below are the eight steps that, when followed, can go a long way to cleaning up the computer mess:

- *Step 1 – Identify computer problem.* The three diagnostic tools described earlier in this chapter (smell, analytical, and probing tests) are effective in problem identification. As previously stated, until the problem is identified the solution cannot be developed. Management must remember that data processing people tend to be optimistic and therefore frequently downplay the severity of problems. Close management scrutiny of the data processing area, together with the proper use of the diagnostic tools, will help uncover many data processing problems before they become serious.

- *Step 2 – Determine impact of problem.* Until the significance of a problem is known, it cannot be adequately addressed. If an automobile engine starts making noise, the driver has a decision to make – stop the car immediately, drive to the nearest service station, or wait until the next scheduled maintenance takes place. Should the driver misestimate the severity of the problem and select the wrong alternative, a disaster can occur. The disaster may be serious engine damage, personal injury, breakdown on a deserted highway, heart attack due to anger and frustration, or an unnecessary costly repair bill. In most

NO.	STEP	PURPOSE
1.	Identify computer problem	Define problem to be solved
2.	Determine impact of problem	Determine whether problem warrants being addressed by management
3.	Identify management objective	State the objective to be accomplished that will reduce or eliminate the problem
4.	Identify solution criteria	State what will determine that the objective has been accomplished
5.	Brainstorm and analyze	List the solution alternatives
6.	Select solution	Pick the best solution
7.	Evaluate road blocks	Determine that the selected solution has a high probability of being successful
8.	Develop implementation plan	Create a plan of action for implementing the selected solution

Figure 9. Steps in problem-solving.

instances knowing the severity of the computer problem will determine the type and timeliness of action. This can frequently be determined by asking the following questions:

1. If the problem is not fixed in five minutes, what will happen to the business?
2. If the problem is not fixed within one hour, what will happen to the business?
3. If the problem is not fixed within one day, what will happen to the business?
4. If the problem is not fixed within one week, what will happen to the business?
5. If the problem is not fixed within one month, what will happen to the business?

- *Step 3 — Identify management objective.* Once the problem and its severity have been determined, management must state the type of corrective action it desires. This corrective action should be expressed in terms of a management objective. In other words, the solution should be some specific task to be accomplished by the data processing project team. The management objectives expressed in general terms are stated in Figure 5. These objectives are eliminate, rearrange, change, combine, improve, comply, and revise. These generalized objectives need to be customized for the specific problem and then given to the group responsible for implementing the objective.

- *Step 4 — Identify solution criteria.* To ensure that the solution meets management's objectives, management must state the criteria by which it will judge the solution. For example, if you gave someone the assignment of situating a sales office, you might give him the criteria by which a successful sales office would be judged, such as within fifty miles of a million or more people, near a major railroad and airport, rentable at a cost not exceeding $5 per square foot, etc. Having these criteria, the individual responsible for the solution will know whether or not he has developed a solution acceptable to management.

- *Step 5 — Brainstorm and analyze.* The implementation team should attempt to identify all the possible solution alternatives. This can be done by first brainstorming, which gives everyone involved an opportunity to express solution alternatives. This should be done before any analysis is undertaken, so that every party has an opportunity to be heard without criticism. It is extremely important that all alternatives be identified, so that those involved cannot say that there was another solution that was not considered. Once the alternatives have been identified, they should be analyzed to determine:

— Cost to implement, effort to implement, impact on people if implemented, impact on systems when implemented
— Method of implementation
— Resources needed to implement

- *Step 6 — Select solution.* From the series of alternatives, the project team should select what appears to be the best solution. This can be accomplished through voting, or identifying the attributes of all the solutions, weighting or ranking the attributes to represent their relative importance, and then evaluating each alternative on those attributes. The alternative that satisfies the most attributes the best should be the selected solution.
- *Step 7 — Evaluate roadblocks.* Solutions work only when all parties involved want them to work. Solutions sabotage is a common characteristic of computer applications that fail. Most of the reasons a solution will not work can be easily identified if time is taken to identify those roadblocks. In this step, all the reasons the selected solution won't work should be identified. Countermeasures need to be developed for each of those roadblocks. If after consideration of a roadblock no realistic countermeasure can be found, and the roadblock appears serious, then that alternative should be dropped and another considered. It is far better to implement a solution that will work, even though it is not the preferred solution, than to implement the preferred solution and find it won't work.
- *Step 8 — Develop implementation plan.* The implementation plan is the plan of action for implementing the selected solution. The remaining chapters in the book provide information to help develop good implementation plans for the areas addressed. The diagnostic tools point to the appropriate chapter. That information should be studied and included in the appropriate plan of action.

WHAT TO DO UNTIL THE DOCTOR CALLS?

The problem many managers face is how to keep the patient alive until the doctor comes. In some instances, the solution will be to hire a new data processing manager, scrap an existing application and acquire or develop a new one, or perhaps the even more drastic step of contracting with a service bureau to perform all the data processing services. As any manager knows, many of these solutions take time to plan and time to implement. In the meantime, the organization cannot stop doing business.

When a serious computer problem exists, management has two challenges. The first is overcoming the immediate problem and satisfying an immediate processing need. Second is to develop and implement a long-term solution to the problem. Unfortunately, if the short-term solution is not satisfied there may be no long-term solution. Though the business may survive, the individual manager may not.

There is generally no easy solution to a severe computer mess. Chapters 3 through 12 provide some short-term solutions for some specific problems. These short-term solutions generally center on one of the following survival strategies:

- *Survival strategy 1 — Retreat to a manual processing environment.* If the computer solution falls significantly short of the desired objectives, it may be far better to scrap the system and revert to manual processing. Although this may require hiring temporary help and swallowing a little pride, it may be cheaper in the long run than attempting to tough it out with a problem computer application.
- *Survival strategy 2 — Overwhelm with manpower.* Some problems may be solvable by throwing enough resources at them. For example, if inputs are manually checked, programs handheld while operating, and outputs scrutinized and changed where necessary, the results may be usable. The staff cannot live long in this mode, of course, but its implementation may alleviate a temporary problem long enough to install a longer range fix.
- *Survival strategy 3 — Shoot and replace the enemy.* In some instances, there is no alternative but to get rid of the troublemakers.

If a programmer can't hack it or the manager can't manage, it may be better to eliminate that individual on the spot. The replacements can be people readily available on the job market, some of whom may be able to start tomorrow, or consultants. Consulting help can be available from data processing service bureaus, computer vendors, public accounting firms, and independent consultants.

No strategy is too drastic if it helps the business survive a crisis. In some instances, a survival strategy may be needed to avoid a disaster. Data processing is a field that can degrade quickly. Therefore, it behooves management, when a problem appears, to act decisively and quickly.

CLEANUP RULE
He who fights and runs away will live to fight another day.

Part 2
How to Get Your Computer Back on Track

There are never enough resources to do the job right the first time, but always enough to correct a problem. Learning from your own experiences and from those who have traveled the cleanup path ahead of you should put your derailed computer goals back on track.

3
SOLVING AN ORGANIZATIONAL DISPUTE

There is a tendency with a technical problem to look for a technical solution. Unfortunately, computers rarely make mistakes; people frequently make mistakes. The real culprit in 99 out of 100 computer problems is people.

A partner in one of the Big Eight CPA firms once stated that he never knew a computer that embezzled or stole from its employer. His argument was that management should direct its controls at people and not at machines. We read wild stories about what computers do, but as of this date none has ever been convicted of a crime. After all, how could *Time Magazine's* man of the year of 1983 possibly steal from its employer?

This chapter deals with the people problem from an organizational perspective. It explains why the computer poses some unique organizational challenges and then offers suggestions on how to overcome shortcomings in traditional organizational structure. This chapter, like those that follow, explains the symptoms of organizational problems, how to diagnose those diseases, and then how to implement effective cures. The chapter also provides survival tactics while you are waiting for the cure to take effect.

THE ORGANIZATIONAL CHALLENGE POSED BY THE COMPUTER

Prior to the introduction of computers, most organizations established and operated dedicated systems. A dedicated system is a processing procedure under which the control of the data and the processing rules remains in a single organizational unit, *dedicated* meaning that the organizational unit responsible for the application "owns" the application. For example, the accounts receivable department owns the accounts receivable ledger and processing associated with that ledger.

Many of the early computer applications were dedicated applications. In larger organizations, single departments frequently had their own computer and processed their own data on that computer. Gradually, these dedicated systems became integrated systems. In integrated systems, data flows from system to system to system.

The major difference between dedicated and integrated systems is the need for standardization, reliability, and consistency. The user of information created by another organizational entity must be able to rely upon the integrity, reliability, and consistency of data provided by another department.

The integrated systems require more standardization and control than do dedicated systems. For example, in a dedicated system if I want to use a five-position number to indicate customer I can do that, and another department can use a seven-position number to indicate that same customer. This does not cause a problem until the two systems are integrated and customer number is passed from system to system.

As technology advances, integrated systems are beginning to use common data through a concept called *data base technology*. Data base is a central repository for data, just as a central filing area is a central repository for paper documents. If one can visualize the difference in control between a local filing system and a centralized filing system, one can start to visualize the type of control that is needed over a centralized data base.

As technology progresses, so does the need for control. The dedicated system was merely an extension of the processing of a single department. An integrated data base system combines the processing needs, and problems, of the entire organization into a single processing system. Without centralized control, a real computer mess can evolve. Advanced technology and control must go hand-in-hand.

The problem in controlling a centralized, computerized business application is illustrated in Figure 10. This illustration shows that the typical organizational structure is vertical. The president is in charge of the organization; he delegates responsibility and authority to vice presidents, who further delegate to managers, who delegate to staff. Computerized business applications, however, are horizontal. Information flows between organizational units horizontally, as opposed to the vertical organizational structure.

Let's look at the type of problem that this might cause an organization. Let's assume that our computerized business application is

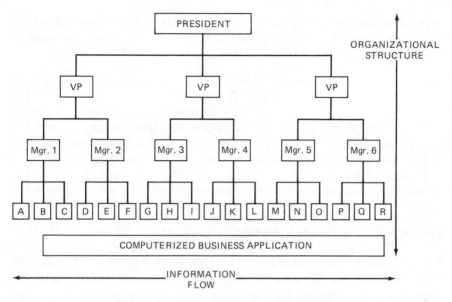

Figure 10. EDP organizational challenge.

an order entry, billing, receivables inventory management, and inventory replenishment system. The order drives the system, meaning that it creates the shipment of product, the billing, the receivables, and the reorder of stock. Let's further assume that manager 1 is the order entry manager and manager 6 is the inventory replenishment manager. We said that inventory was replenished based upon orders.

A typical problem that might occur is that manager 6 needs some special order entry information, let's say commitments in addition to orders, so that the proper on-hand inventory can be maintained. If manager 1 decides that that change would be a significant increase in workload for his employees, manager 1 may decide not to enter that additional information. If manager 1 and manager 6 have a dispute over a common computer system, the only individual that can resolve that dispute is the president of the organization. Should the problem be between employees *A* and *R,* employee *R* would go to manager 6, who would go to his vice president, who would go to the president of the organization, who in turn must go to manager 1's vice president to talk to manager 1 to talk to employee *A.* This process is unworkable because the president of an organization does not want to be the project leader of the computer systems. However, without someone taking an active role, costly organizational disputes can evolve and fester over a period of years at a significant cost to the organization.

CLEANUP RULE

It has frequently been stated that a camel is a horse built by a committee. If your computer systems are built by a committee, you may be processing camels on your computer instead of thoroughbred applications.

SYMPTOMS OF AN ORGANIZATIONAL DISEASE

Symptoms are the outward sign of a problem. They are the characteristics that can be used to diagnose a problem. Unfortunately, the same symptoms may be representative of two or more illnesses.

Let's look at a patient who walks into a hospital complaining about pains in his arm. To the casual observer, it is the arm that hurts, and the trouble could be a muscle or ligament problem. If the symptom is treated quickly, the arm may be bandaged and put into a sling and the patient sent home. More thorough treatment might lead to further diagnosis, which might reveal that the patient is having a heart problem and that the pain in the arm is a symptom of a heart problem, rather than damage to the arm itself.

In a computer installation, the same diagnosis can occur from a symptom. For example, a project over budget is a symptom of a problem. The easy diagnosis is to blame the project team for mismanagement and reprimand it for its inability to complete the project within the budget. Further investigation, however, may diagnose the true cause of the project being over budget as:

- Improper tools provided to develop a realistic estimate
- Project staffed with the wrong skills
- Uncooperative user
- Change in requirements since the estimate was developed
- Inadequate staffing mix, meaning that too many people were assigned at the wrong part of the project
- Turnover of project personnel

Symptoms are important because, properly utilized, they lead to the cause of the problem. However, management is cautioned that symptoms can be abused as well as used. It is in the avoidance of the abuse of the use of symptoms that the need for in-depth analysis is stressed.

The symptoms commonly associated with organizational problems are listed in Figure 11 and described below (Note that the severity of the symptom is also indicated in Figure 11. The severity is relational, meaning that those symptoms indicated with a high severity are more serious than the symptoms indicated to be medium and low.):

- *Symptom 1 − Inability of staff to diagnose cause of problem.* If you have ever had the opportunity to talk to both parties in an automobile accident, you may leave the scene of the accident confused. Listening to the parties involved, you would assume they were in different accidents. The same situation occurs with computer problems. Management listens to all the parties involved, but after the discussion is concluded management has no clearer idea of what the problem is before the discussion than after. This does not mean that the individual parties are not emphatic about the cause of the problem, it means that two or more parties are equally emphatic about the cause of the problem, but the stated causes are different.
- *Symptom 2 − Unassigned responsibility.* Large integrated computer systems may involve many organizational units. Although the project may be under the supervision of a single organizational unit, tasks need to be performed by the various involved units. However, either the supervising unit does not feel it has authority to make an assignment outside the area of its responsibility, assumes the other unit will handle its own responsibility, or may be unaware of the need to assign a responsibility. The end result is that a task falls between the cracks. Examples of such tasks include:
  − Responsibility for generalized data elements, such as customer number, product number, and vendor number
  − Error correction and reentry
  − Verification of master information, such as customer name and address, correct spelling of product name
  − Notifying users and customers of problems
  − Verifying integrity of computer files

NO.	SYMPTOM	EXPLANATION	SEVERITY
1.	Inability of staff to diagnose cause of problems	Two or more groups express different causes for the same problem	High
2.	Unassigned responsibility	There is some aspect of the computer system for which no one has been assigned responsibility	High
3.	High turnover in EDP	The data processing department is experiencing a turnover rate of 20 percent or greater per year	High
4.	Excessive computer time	The computer resources are under-utilized	Medium
5.	Inadequate computer time	The organization does not have sufficient computer resources to process the current workload	Medium
6.	Behind schedule	A project under development or the operation of a computer application is behind schedule	Medium
7.	Over budget	The development or maintenance of an application system or the cost of operating an application system is over the estimated budget	Medium
8.	Important projects delayed	Projects important to the business cannot be implemented when desired	Medium
9.	EDP uninformed of change	The user has incorporated some change in processing, but has not notified the data processing department to change the computer systems accordingly	Low
10.	User uninformed of change	The data processing department has made a change to the computer system, but has not informed the user of that change	Low

Figure 11. Symptoms of an organizational problem.

- *Symptom 3 – High turnover in EDP.* Staff and management in the data processing organization leave either the data processing department or the organization. Generally, a turnover of greater than 20 percent in a year is indicative of problems, unless the individuals are leaving for better positions within the organization or are transferred by the organization. Reasons for leaving the organization should be ignored.
- *Symptom 4 – Excessive computer time.* The amount of computer capacity far exceeds the processing requirements. In a well-run computer installation production should account for two-thirds to three-fourths of available capacity.
- *Symptom 5 – Inadequate computer time.* The capacity available on the computer is inadequate to handle the processing requirements of the organization. This normally occurs when production exceeds 80 percent of capacity, requiring the data processing department to complete its work during nonscheduled hours. Note that short periods of lack of computer capacity should not be considered a problem, such as month-end or year-end processing binds.
- *Symptom 6 – Behind schedule.* The established target dates or times for project development or operation have not been met. Note that reasonable tolerances should be considered before a project is stated to be behind schedule.
- *Symptom 7 – Over budget.* Computer project development, maintenance, or operation exceeds the budgeted amount for that project. Note that reasonable tolerances should be considered before a project is stated to be over budget.
- *Symptom 8 – Important projects delayed.* The prioritization for implementing or operating projects is usually negotiated between users and the data processing department. Unfortunately, the squeaky wheel usually gets the oil. This may mean that certain users monopolize the resources, delaying projects considered to be high priority by senior management.
- *Symptom 9 – EDP uninformed of change.* Users introduce processing requirements, but fail to inform the data processing department of the change, so its impact on the automated applications can be assessed and changes made accordingly. Note that if the change does not affect the computer system the communication may be unnecessary.
- *Symptom 10 – User uninformed of change.* The data processing department changes the automated application, but fails to

notify the user that the change has been placed into production. Note that except for routine operational changes, such as the installation of a new version of an operating system, the user should be informed of all changes, due to the risk of problems occurring and the user not being alerted to that risk.

ORGANIZATIONAL PROBLEM DIAGNOSTIC PROCESS

The recommended diagnostic approach for organizational problems is probing. This is an investigative technique with senior management as the investigators. The objective is to determine whether or not the cause of the problem symptoms is organizational in nature.

The investigator should determine which symptoms from Figure 11 are of concern. These symptoms should then be investigated through probing with the involved organizational units. The net result of this probing should be the identification of the cause, and thus the ability to select the appropriate solution.

An Organizational Problem Diagnostic Checklist is provided in Figure 12 to aid the manager in the analysis process. The checklist is used by first identifying the symptom numbers of concern from Figure 11. This number is located in the symptom number column of Figure 12. The items following that symptom are the items that should be probed by the investigator. If a no response is provided, it can be assumed that that symptom does not represent an organizational problem. If a yes response is given, there is a high probability that an organizational problem exists. If the item is not applicable, the user should check the not applicable (NA) column. Yes responses, and questionable no responses should be clarified or explained in the comments column of Figure 12.

The checklists are designed to be answered by the user of the checklist. This means that the investigator will perform sufficient investigation to be able to answer the item yes or no. The items are not designed to be asked of third parties and to have the user mark the third party's response on the checklist. The investigation will normally take a series of questions and examination of project information in order for the item to be appropriately answered.

If one or more items under each symptom are answered yes, there is a high probability that an organizational problem is causing the computer mess. The more yes responses, the greater the probability of an organizational problem. For those organizational problems,

SYMPTOM NO.	ITEM	RESPONSE			SOLUTION REF. NO.	COMMENTS
		YES	NO	NA		
1	Has the organization failed to develop a formal method for documenting computer problems?				3	
1	Has the organization failed to assign responsibility for each computer application to a specific individual?				2	
1	Has the organization failed to assign the responsibility for problem diagnosis?				2	
2	Has the organization failed to assign responsibility for each computer file to a single individual?				2	
2	Has the organization failed to assign responsibility for the integrity, accuracy, completeness, and security of each data item (data field) to a single individual?				2	
2	Has the organization failed to assign the responsibility for each task in the application system (e.g., preparation of input forms, error correction procedures, processing of output data, etc.) to a single individual?				2	
3	Is there a high turnover among data processing management?				1	
3	Is there a high turnover among data processing technical staff?				2	
3	Does the data processing function have inadequate staff?				4	
4	Is the excessive computer capacity due to unimplemented requests?				3	
4	Is the excessive computer time due to too much hardware?				4	
4	Is the excessive computer time due to an inaccurate volume estimate?				4	
5	Is the inadequate computer time due to inaccurately estimated volumes?				4	
5	Is the inadequate computer time due to the inability to obtain hardware quickly from the vendor?				4	

Figure 12. Organizational problem diagnostic checklist.
(NOTE: Yes responses are indicative of potential computer problems.)

SYMPTOM NO.	ITEM	RESPONSE			SOLUTION REF. NO.	COMMENTS
		YES	NO	NA		
5	Is the inadequate computer time due to users not informing data processing of future workloads?				3	
6	Is computer operations behind schedule?				4	
6	Is computer project development behind schedule?				4	
6	Is the acquisition of hardware and software behind schedule?				4	
7	Is computer operations over budget?				4	
7	Is systems development and maintenance over budget?				4	
7	Is the cost associated with the acquisition of hardware and software over budget?				4	
8	Are projects important to management behind schedule because the prioritization has not been transmitted to the data processing department?				3	
8	Are important projects delayed because of inadequate data processing resources?				4	
8	Are important projects delayed because operating management does not agree on organizationwide priorities?				1	
9	Can changes be made without a formal change request form?				3	
9	Are formal lines of communication non-existent between the user and the data processing department?				3	
9	Has the organization failed to assign responsibilities for each computer task to a single individual?				2	
10	Are users unaware when each new version of the application for which they are responsible is implemented?				3	
10	Can changes to application systems be made without authorization by the responsible user?				2	
10	Are users unable to set priorities for the sequence in which changes to computer applications will be made?				4	

Figure 12. Organizational problem diagnostic checklist (cont.)
(Note: Yes responses are indicative of potential computer problems.)

one of four solutions is recommended. The solution reference number is listed on Figure 12 and described in Figure 13 for organizational problems.

ORGANIZATIONAL PROBLEM SOLUTIONS

The solution to a problem begins with a managerial concern, which leads to the identification of symptoms, which must be analyzed to identify the cause of the problem, which in turn points to the solution. For every managerial data processing concern, this process should be repeated.

There are four basic causes of organizational problems. The diagnostic checklist has pointed to these causes, as well as the solutions. The four causes, coupled with the logic leading to a solution, are listed in Figure 13 and described below:

- *Cause 1 — Improper organizational structure.* The organizational structure has not been rearranged to complement the characteristics of automation.
- *Cause 2 — Inadequate assignment of responsibilities.* As the methods of doing work are resystematized, the assignment of those responsibilities changes. When the responsibilities get out of synchronization with the systems, problems occur.
- *Cause 3 — Lack of adequate communication.* The industrial psychologists tell us that poor communication is the cause of most problems. Communications with a computer department are frequently difficult due to the technical language and preciseness of the data processing profession.
- *Cause 4 — Insufficient EDP planning.* Many of the problems associated with data processing can be directly related to the lack of planning. In many organizations where the DP department plans, it fails to integrate those plans into the organizational plans, resulting in DP going in one direction, while the business is going in another direction.

The methodology for diagnosing and solving a computer problem was explained in Figure 5. This figure explained how to identify the cause of the problem, which good business practice that cause violated, and then proposed a generalized solution to the problem.

NO.	CAUSE OF PROBLEM		PRINCIPLE VIOLATED	RECOMMENDED SOLUTION	
	SPECIFIC	GENERAL		GENERAL	SPECIFIC
1	Improper organizational structure	Inconvenient location	Smooth flow	Rearrange	Establish a business system planning committee
2	Inadequate assignment of responsibilities	Fragmented, improper skills	Productivity	Change, combine	Assign project sponsors
3	Lack of adequate communication	Complicated	Simplicity	Improve	Establish review boards
4	Insufficient EDP planning	Costly	Simplicity	Improve	Develop short- and long-range EDP plans and integrate into organizational business plan

Figure 13. Organizational problem solution matrix.

Using this approach, we can develop a solution based upon the specific cause of the organizational problem.

Figure 13 shows that the specific organizational cause of the problem can be categorized into the general cause of computer problem as discussed in Figure 5. For the specific organizational problem of "improper organizational structure," the general problem is an inconvenient location for the work. This violates the principle of "smooth flow" of work. The general solution is to "rearrange" the activities, which can best be accomplished by using the solution of establishing a business system planning committee. Following this same logic, all four causes of organizational problems lead to specific organizational solutions. Using the solution matrix, the manager can select a specific solution or solutions to solve problems originating from organizational difficulties.

An explanation of and a suggested method for implementing each of the recommended solutions follows:

- *Solution 1 — Establish a business system planning committee.* A business system planning committee is a committee that comprises the key members of senior management. In all but the very large organizations, it is chaired by the president of the corporation. The responsibility of the business systems planning committee is to establish data processing policy and priorities, with emphasis on priorities.

  After establishment, the business system planning committee rarely meets more than once a quarter. Because the members of the committee comprise all areas of the business, they will know what data processing jobs need to be accomplished in their areas of responsibility. All these jobs will be listed, together with the estimated resources for completion. The committee then prioritizes the jobs and gives them to the data processing department to be completed within that priority ranking. If a major data processing policy, such as changing hardware vendors, needs to be made, the business system planning committee would also establish or approve that policy.

- *Solution 2 — Assign project sponsors.* A project sponsor is someone from outside data processing who is assigned responsibility for a data processing project. This individual normally has the following three responsibilities for each computer project:

- To pay for the project
- To define the project specifications and the criteria by which the successful implementation of the project will be judged
- To ensure that the project is completed right the first time, i.e., to ensure that the quality of the project is satisfactory.

A project sponsor is normally a member of senior management. The higher in the organizational structure the sponsor is located, the more time, attention, and effort that will be devoted to the successful implementation of that project. The objective of the sponsor is to ensure that the responsibility for the successful completion of a data processing project resides with a member of management outside the data processing function. Another major function of the sponsor is to establish and run a review board charged with ensuring the quality of the implemented project (see solution 3).

- *Solution 3 – Establish review boards.* A review board is a group of people having vested interests in the successful completion of a computer project. The members of the board come from all organizational areas having an interest in the computer project. The responsibility of the review board is to ensure that the project is not implemented until it meets a minimum quality level. The review board should be chaired by the project sponsor.

The specific responsibilities of a review board are:

- Identify the criteria that, if achieved, will indicate a successful project.
- Select points in the system development process to review the quality of the system.
- Develop or acquire a review methodology.
- Conduct periodic quality control reviews.
- Prepare reports on the level of quality of the project.
- Formally state the level of quality of the system prior to implementation, whether or not the board believes the project should be implemented.

- *Solution 4 – Develop short- and long-range EDP plans.* A short-range EDP plan is a one-year plan, and a long-range plan is a three-, five-, or ten-year plan. The DP plan should project costs, personnel, workload, technology, and strategies. The data processing plan should be a subset of the organizational business plan. Generally, it is not possible to develop a realistic data processing plan until the organization's business plan has been formalized.

One member of the data processing department should have responsibility for planning. This need not be a full-time function. That individual should also be part of the organization's planning team. The final DP plan should be integrated into and be a part of the organization's business plan.

IMPEDIMENTS TO IMPLEMENTING ORGANIZATIONAL SOLUTIONS

A major impediment to almost any solution is resistance to change. Even if the current organizational structure is lacking, people may be reluctant to adopt a new organizational structure. One DP manager said, "Never wish for a new king, the old one is bad enough!"

The specific impediments for each of the four solutions, together with countermeasures, are discussed below:

- *Solution establishing a business system planning committee.* The impediments to a business system's planning committee are:

  - Management does not have enough time — Time spent avoiding problems saves time spent correcting them. Planning is also a more enjoyable experience than firefighting. Senior management must recognize its EDP responsibilities and act accordingly.
  - Senior management lacks the technical expertise to plan data processing — Planning and establishing business priorities is not a technical function, it's a business function. This is equivalent to saying you can't drive a car because you don't know how the internal combustion engine works. Senior management is far more successful in establishing business priorities for data processing than the technical data processing management is in establishing those same business priorities. Let management do what it does best and technicians do what they do best.
  - That's what we hired the DP manager to do! — The business system planning committee should not get involved in the

technical aspects of data processing, only the business uses of data processing.

- *Solution to assign project sponsors.*   The impediments to assigning project sponsors are:

  - A senior manager does not have enough time to be a project sponsor — The role does not have to be time-consuming, but it must be control-oriented. If no manager cares enough about a project to be willing to spend the time to be that project's sponsor, then perhaps the project should not be implemented. Experience has shown that projects without strong management support tend to be the problem applications.
  - NonDP managers lack the skills needed to oversee the implementation of a data processing project — True, but the skills are obtainable without large expenditures of time and effort. This impediment is a real one, but one that the interested manager will spend time to overcome. Most of the mainframe vendors offer one-week courses that provide the basic skills to become a project sponsor.
  - The project involves several areas and should be run by a committee — Camels are built by committees. Somebody must be in charge, and it shouldn't be a committee, it should be a single individual. The chief executive officer can neither hang nor praise a committee, but can provide an individual his just rewards.

- *Solution to establish review boards.*   If only one solution could be picked, it should be the review board. There is no greater learning experience than living with a computer project during its development and implementation phases. However, the impediments to establishing a review board include:

  - It's a Big Brother tactic by senior management — Review boards are not designed to be policemen, but rather to be participants in the project development. Not only does the board review, but it involves those people in the review who have a vested interest in the success of the project. Therefore, as the reviewers see problems, they can also become a part of the solution.

- Review boards delay implementation — Just the opposite is true. Problems corrected in the early stages of development require one-tenth or less effort than the resources consumed correcting that same problem during the latter stages of development. True, a review board may extend requirements, but the rest of the development process should be shortened.

- *Solution to develop short- and long-range EDP plans.* The impediments to data processing planning include:

  - Data processing is too new to plan — Many believe that planning should be grounded on past experience. Without planning, businesses may not be able to afford the cost of that experience. Long-range plans may be more difficult in the early years of data processing, but short-range plans are essential. The lack of planning is usually associated with the high cost of handling emergency conditions.
  - It is more important to complete the current backlog of work than to plan — Perhaps the reason for the backlog is the lack of planning. Industrywide data processing professionals do not appear to enjoy planning, nor do they do it well. Managerial assistance may be needed in this area.
  - Planning cannot occur because the users do not know what they want — This is a valid impediment. If the data processing group cannot plan because of the lack of input information, then the planning problem lies outside the data processing function. Management should address that first and the data processing planning second.

ORGANIZATIONAL SURVIVAL TACTICS

Problems need to be addressed quickly. Organizational structures change slowly. This action gap must be closed with survival tactics.

When businesses encounter data processing organizational problems, the survival tactics that have proved successful include:

1. Senior management intervention — Under this tactic a member of senior management in effect takes over the operation of the data processing department. Although the senior managers cannot direct the technical aspects of the functioning

of the department, they can direct the business aspects of the department. This includes establishing priorities, planning, decision making, hiring and firing staff, resolving disputes with users, authorizing overtime and additional assistance, and acquiring more hardware and purchased software. The clout of a senior officer may be needed to instigate policy and direction changes, as well as obtain on-the-spot managerial decisions.

2. Change managers — If the data processing manager appears unable to manage the function, the manager should be replaced. This should be an on-the-spot decision, and when it is made the company officer should walk the manager to the door and then return personal property by mail. The officer can run the department, the senior data processing person left can run the department, or a consultant can be hired to run the department until a manager can be located. Sometimes this shock effect awakens a sleeping giant, and things begin to happen within the data processing function.

3. Establish review task forces — For each project or area in trouble, management can form an ad hoc task force to oversee and assist in the implementation of that project. This is a short-term solution using existing managerial talent from other areas to help overcome data processing shortcomings. If the task forces are established, their role and responsibility should be clearly stated and communicated to all parties.

CLEANUP RULE

The lack of action is a direct cause of most failures. It is the predominating error in every walk of life. Organizational structures should be built to facilitate action, not impede it.

4
SOLVING A VENDOR PROBLEM

The introduction of data processing into an organization is accompanied by the introduction of vendors. These vendors produce the hardware, software, and services needed to operate an effective data processing function. The vendors can be a boon or a bane to the operation of the data processing function.

Data processing vendors are considered by many to be part of the priesthood of the technicrats. And yet many of the vendors' personnel may be "used car salesmen" in a different-colored coat. The myriad of promises made, if fully believed, may help lead your organization down the path of a gigantic computer mess. Unfortunately, both management and the in-house technical staff may be taken in by vendor promises.

This chapter explains how to diagnose a vendor-related problem. It then explains how to transpose that problem into a workable solution. Organizations may have more leverage with vendors than with their own staff because of the storehouse of resources the vendor has available to help bail a client out of a problem.

THE DOS AND DON'TS OF VENDOR RELATIONS

Good vendor relations are developed; they do not exist naturally. The objective of the vendor is to sell product. Everything the vendor does must be considered in relationship to the vendor objective of selling product. There is nothing wrong with this objective as long as the buyer receives quality product and reasonable service with that product.

Organizations should develop a policy for dealing with computer vendors. These vendors may have a unique relationship with the organization. The computer may become so involved with the day-to-day business that the organization cannot function unless the computer is operational. In many instances, it will take the devotion and help of the vendor to ensure the reliability of processing of the computer.

Six policy considerations are recommended for developing a computer vendor policy. These good vendor relation principles are put in the format of dos and don'ts of dealing with vendors (see Figure 14).

These six principles of good vendor relations work. A brief explanation of the dos and don'ts follows:

1. *Ensure that sales personnel are adequately qualified.* The vendor sales person not only sells product, but should serve as a consultant and interface with those vendor individuals who can make things happen. In many dealings with vendors, the sales person is never dealt with after the product is acquired. For example, after you buy a new automobile your future relationships are primarily with the service department. This may not be true with a computer vendor sales person.

   You should insist on dealing with a sales person you have faith in. The sales person should not be someone you constantly argue with or pester to get things accomplished. The types of traits that you should demand in a vendor sales person include:

   — An understanding of data processing principles and concepts
   — An in-depth knowledge of vendor products
   — The authority to take reasonable action
   — The ability to speak for vendors
   — A knowledge or at least an interest in your business

   If the sales person assigned to you does not meet these qualifications, request a different one. If a vendor can't supply you with a good sales person, choose another vendor.

2. *Appoint an official vendor contact.* The vendor should know whom to contact within your organization. Vendors with no previous experience may call on anyone, but once a relationship has been established the vendor should know whom to contact. Once this relationship has been established, vendors should not be permitted to go elsewhere in the organization without the approval of the primary contact. It is recommended that senior management be given a list of vendors with which the data processing group is negotiating,

THE DOS	THE DON'TS
1. Demand a sales person you have faith in	1. Argue with the vendor's sales staff
2. Appoint an official vendor contact	2. Permit the vendor to go to senior management
3. Put all promises in writing	3. Accept "under-the-board" promises of future help
4. Require references	4. Accept references supplied by the vendor
5. Deal exclusively with a quality vendor	5. Shop solely on price
6. Maintain and use records of past work for a vendor	6. Believe things will get better in the future

Figure 14. Good vendor relations.

or has a contract with. If those vendors attempt to go to senior management, they should be sharply discouraged by senior management. If the practice persists, the vendor should be asked to either replace that sales person, or consider the account lost from a sales perspective.

3. *Put everything in the contract.* One of the old songs talks about "promises, promises." Promises by a vendor are just that — promises. If they are kept, the organization should consider it a bonus, but if they are not kept an organization should not be disappointed unless those promises were stipulated in the contract. Legal counsel will advise you that oral promises mean nothing, that the relation with the vendor will be judged solely by the written contract. In fact, many contracts explicitly state that anything not included in the written contract is not to be considered a promise by the vendor. Some sales personnel will state that though they couldn't get some type of service included in the contract they will make sure you get it if you sign the contract. If a sales person makes this "under-the-board" promise, ask:

   — What happens if the sales person leaves the vendor or gets transferred?
   — What happens at a later time if the vendor's supervisor refuses to let that sales person provide these extra services?

4. *Deal only with established vendors.* One of the early lessons learned in data processing is not to pay the price to "debug" a vendor's product. This means that the first few users of a product usually encounter more than an average number of problems. They in effect become the quality control function for the vendor. In the early days of computers, these sites were frequently distinguished as *data sites* to make the agony of debugging the product sound like a unique benefit offered by the vendor. Too many of these debugging benefits can put your organization out of business.

   You should require references from other customers using the same product or service you are negotiating for. You should ask the vendor for a customer list from which you will pick a representative number of references. It is reasonable for the vendor to insist that you not contact that customer until the vendor has obtained prior approval for the contact. However, you should not accept a list of references provided by the vendor. You should expect these references to be the best the vendor has to offer and thus to be biased toward the vendor's product.

5. *Use quality vendors.* Many data processing managers in the early days of data processing used to say, "If I deal with IBM and the system doesn't work, my management will think I have done the best I can, but if I deal with other than IBM and the system doesn't work, management will think I chose the wrong vendor." This is not meant to be a testimonial for the IBM Corporation, but rather the importance many people place on dealing with a quality vendor. Quality must be demonstrable through performance, quality control procedures, etc. Quality is not a word in an advertising brochure, but rather a guarantee of the expected performance should you buy the vendor product, such as 98 percent uptime, less than one defect per program per year, etc. Organizations that shop solely on price in the data processing field usually get just what they pay for — junk!

6. *Keep records on the vendors.* Making a mistake in choosing a vendor is a shame, but to choose that same vendor a second time is a sin. Organizations should maintain records on past relationships with vendors, both vendors with whom they contract and vendors with whom they negotiate. Many times, a good vendor will not be chosen for a contract, but based on negotiating performance should be considered for a future contract.

Organizations that believe things will get better in the future are normally disappointed. Past experience is an excellent predictor of future performance. Organizations that deal with a small group of highly reliable vendors are almost always better off than those organizations that continually shop around for a better product.

CLEANUP RULE

In today's computer field, vendors rise and fall like rockets. If you want good products, be sure the vendor you select has had sufficient flying experience so that you will not be selecting a product with a high probability of crashing.

SYMPTOMS OF A VENDOR PROBLEM

Computer vendors are frequently colleagues and friends of the data processing staff. In many organizations, there are few people who can discuss the technical aspects of data processing. Therefore, the vendors become confidants and contacts with the outside world. There is nothing wrong with this relationship, except that it may break down the barriers of knowing who is working for whom.

Senior management should also be aware that vendors frequently act as employment agencies for data processing personnel. This is an unpaid service, but one that can be extremely important to the individual. It can also be important to the vendor, because placing the vendor's equipment may be contingent upon getting the right manager or staff members to operate that equipment. Little can be done to prevent this practice, because it is one done for friendship and not for a fee. Still, it shows the importance of senior management overseeing vendor contracts and vendor relationships.

The close relationship between the data processing staff and the vendors may mask potential vendor problems. The data processing staff may work with the vendor to help overcome problems that are the responsibility of the vendor to fix. Therefore, it is highly probable that the business is paying to debug, detect, and remedy vendor problems.

The vendor problem symptoms that management should look for are listed in Figure 15 and described below:

- *Symptom 1 — Behind schedule.* The actual costs exceed the budgeted or contracted cost for a vendor-produced product. Most likely, the increase in cost can be readily explained, but it is still symptomatic of a potential problem. Again, it needs to be emphasized that these are symptoms, not causes of a problem. If the cause can be readily explained to the satisfaction of management, no further action will be required.

   The reasons that many services exceed budget estimates include:

   - Data processing changed the requirements after the order was placed

NO.	SYMPTOM	EXPLANATION	SEVERITY
1.	Behind schedule	The promised delivery date for vendor hardware, software, or service has been delayed	High
2.	Inadequate computer time	The capacity provided by the vendor hardware and software is inadequate to meet processing requirements (note that inadequacy should be due to inability of vendor hardware or software to perform as specified)	High
3.	No one accepts responsibility for a problem	Two or more vendor products are intercoupled, or vendor product intercoupled with in-house-developed system, with vendor refusing to accept responsibility for a problem	High
4.	Purchased application requires extensive in-house modification	The cost of installing an application far exceeds the cost of purchasing the application	High
5.	Over budget	The agreed price for a product is exceeded for any one of a variety of reasons stated by the vendor	Medium
6.	Vendor contract dispute	There is a disagreement between the vendor and the business over the meaning of a clause in a contract	Medium
7.	Needed services for a product not provided by the contract	After a product has been acquired, an uncontracted-for service, such as updating an application for a new version of an operating system, results in an extra charge by the vendor	Medium
8.	Ordered hardware will not be available when needed	The business needs hardware by a specific date and is told that the vendor cannot deliver the hardware by that date	Medium
9.	Excessive computer time	The acquired hardware and software produce much greater processing capacity than is needed by the organization	Low

Figure 15. Symptoms of a vendor problem.

- Increases in vendor products between date of order and date of delivery
- New options offered by a vendor accepted in place of original product
- Vendor services needed, but not provided for in original contract

- *Symptom 2 — Inadequate computer time.* The processing capacity available from computer hardware is dependent upon the mainframe, the mix of input/output devices, and the types and performance of operating software used. This area is highly technical, but the end result is the equivalent to miles per gallon in an automobile. The reasons an automobile may not get the stated miles per gallon can be hidden in technical jargon, but the end result cannot be. If the vendor's products were to deliver some predefined benchmark processing, such as four-second response time, that benchmark can be measured.

  There may not be a short-term solution to increase the computer processing capacity. This is because there may be an inherent flaw in the design of the software or mix of hardware input/output devices attached. In other words, the car just doesn't have it. However, there is a longer term solution, which may be getting rid of the vendor or having the vendor upgrade capacity at no cost to the business.

- *Symptom 3 — No one accepts responsibility for a problem.* Vendors prefer that a customer use their products exclusively. However, this is not always the case. When multiple vendors are involved there may be difficulty in pinpointing the source of a problem. One vendor does not want to diagnose another vendor's problem. This can result in a stalemate for the company, in which each vendor indicates that the cause of a problem is the result of another vendor's product.

- *Symptom 4 — Purchased application requires extensive in-house modification.* If the outputs produced by the computer system fail to satisfy user requirements, those outputs will need to be changed. One method of changing computer-produced outputs is to make that change manually. For example, if an address is wrong, a product is misspelled, an amount accumulated incorrectly, or a total needed is not accumulated, those changes can be made manually. This requires the user to review all computer outputs, identify the errors, and then manually correct them.

Some minor manual adjustments may be necessary as a short-term solution or for emphasis. For example, a user may want to stamp "OVERDUE" in red on an invoice. This type of manual adjustment should not be considered symptomatic of a problem, but rather an economical way to emphasize some aspect of processing. If users are making these changes because of the inability of the computer system to provide that information, however, a serious problem may exist.

- *Symptom 5 — Over budget.* The characteristics of and causes for being over budget closely parallel those of the behind-schedule symptom (see symptom 1). However, budget problems are solvable with extra monies or negotiation, but scheduling problems may not be solvable. Delays in schedule may result in lost competitive advantage, lost opportunity, or delays in receiving expected benefits.

- *Symptom 6 — Vendor contract dispute.* Poorly written contracts are subject to interpretation. Phrases like "provide service within a reasonable time span" really don't say when service will be provided. Reasonable to the computer center may be one hour, but reasonable to the vendor may be one week. Disputes generally represent poorly written contracts.
  The contractual areas most subject to dispute include:

  — Completeness of computer documentation
  — Quality of product delivered
  — Types of services to be provided after the product is delivered
  — Time span in which services will be provided
  — Vendor's willingness to maintain or enhance products after delivery
  — Cost of services not provided for in contract

- *Symptom 7 — Needed services for a product not provided by the contract.* Many parties entering into a contract are optimistic about the performance of the product. Like any other aspect of data processing, this is a period of excitement, sometimes referred to as a *honeymoon* with the vendor. Therefore, the contracts tend to be written assuming that the delivered product will meet the business's requirements.

Vendor services are normally required when the product fails to meet the business's needs. This does not mean that the vendor did not meet the contractual specifications, but rather that, based on what is known now, the product lacks one or more desirable features. The more provisions that can be made for the unexpected, the more satisfactory the contract will be to the business. What is needed is for the contracting parties to brainstorm what can go wrong with the product and then provide provisions in the contract to deal with those contingencies.

- *Symptom 8 — Ordered hardware will not be available when needed.* Most computer products are not bought off the shelf. There is a delay between the time the product is ordered and when it is delivered. With large-scale computers, this delay can be several years. This means that if the data processing manager does not know today the type of hardware that will be needed twelve or twenty-four months in the future, that hardware may not be obtainable when needed. This symptom is almost always attributable to the lack of planning by one or more of the parties involved in data processing.

- *Symptom 9 — Excessive computer time.* It is easy to overbuy computer capacity. The extra cost between two levels of capacity may seem insignificant, and therefore the data processing manager is easily sold this extra capacity. However, it results in the same cost as buying too much inventory or too many office supplies. Those funds expended for unneeded capacity come directly from the bottom-line profitability.

  Management should monitor the number of "CPU hours" used during the month. Most vendors put clocks on their hardware that measure when the computer is being used and when it's not being used. Therefore, even though the computer is physically turned on, the amount of usage can be monitored. If it is less than 50 percent, management should be concerned about overcapacity.

VENDOR PROBLEM DIAGNOSTIC CHECKLIST

A difficult challenge in any technical field is to determine the underlying cause as expressed in problem symptoms. This is a four-step process as follows:

1. Identify symptoms — All the symptoms that represent concerns must be identified.
2. Categorize symptoms — Investigative techniques require that symptoms be expressed in some sort of common terminology or category as part of the analysis process. For example, the symptom might be associated with input problems, vendor problems, etc.
3. Arrange symptoms by category — All the symptoms falling into categories must be put together. It is normally the totality of symptoms that leads to the cause. For example, chest pain alone does not necessarily mean heart attack, but when it is coupled with other symptoms, such as pain down one arm, loss of color, etc., the cause becomes more obvious. Note that the same symptom may have to be categorized into multiple groups.
4. Develop and test hypotheses — Management must speculate on the types of probable causes based on the symptoms and then investigate sufficiently to prove or disprove its hypotheses. If none of the causes turns out to be realistic, then additional cause hypotheses and investigation must be undertaken.

The Vendor Problem Diagnostic Checklist (Figure 16) can be a valuable tool in helping diagnose the problem. This is a series of items to probe in support of the four-step, analytical process just described. This probing should help lead management from the symptoms to the cause of the problem (Step 4 in the above methodology).

The diagnostic checklist begins with the symptom numbers described in Figure 15. A yes response to the item related to a specific symptom indicates a problem. The number in the "solution ref. no." column refers to the most probable cause and solution to the item addressed (see Figure 17). All yes responses should be explained in the comments column. In addition, if a no response is qualified, that too should be explained and may be cause for further investigation.

SOLUTIONS TO VENDOR PROBLEMS

Four solutions are recommended for solving vendor problems. There are many approaches to dealing with vendors, but these four have

SYMPTOM NO.	ITEM	RESPONSE			SOLUTION REF. NO.	COMMENTS
		YES	NO	NA		
1	Is the vendor delay due to data-processing-initiated changes?				2	
1	Are the vendors behind schedule because they apparently have not devoted adequate resources to the contract?				1	
1	Is the vendor behind schedule because the products to be delivered do not work properly?				4	
2	Does the vendor software or hardware fail to meet vendor performance criteria?				4	
2	Is inadequate computer capacity due to the inability to obtain hardware or software when needed?				3	
2	Is inadequate computer capacity caused by poor vendor service?				1	
3	Do vendor contracts fail to specify their problem-solving responsibilities?				2	
3	If more than one vendor is used, is the problem-solving responsibility not assigned to a single vendor?				2	
3	Does the vendor refuse to participate in problem solving if more than one vendor's equipment is interconnected?				1	
4	Does the application developed by the vendor fail to meet the contractual specifications?				2	
4	Have the contractual specifications been changed since the contract was signed?				2	
4	Are changes required to purchased applications because the product fails to meet specifications?				4	
5	Are additional charges assessed because data processing changed a specification?				2	
5	Are additional vendor charges due to needed services that were not included in the original contract?				2	
5	Are the extra charges attributable to lack of attention and resources from the vendor?				1	

Figure 16. Vendor problem diagnostic checklist (cont.).
(NOTE: Yes responses indicate potential computer problems.)

SYMPTOM NO.	ITEM	RESPONSE			SOLUTION REF. NO.	COMMENTS
		YES	NO	NA		
6	Has a contract dispute developed due to an improperly worded contract?				2	
6	Is the contract dispute due to a poor-quality vendor product?				4	
6	Is the contract dispute due to the unwillingness of the vendor to live up to the intent of the contract?				1	
7	Did data processing fail to negotiate for commonly expected computer services, such as maintenance and enhancements?				2	
7	Did the vendor fail to describe the type of support services that would be needed to make the product work effectively?				1	
7	Are additional vendor services required because of the poor quality of the delivered product?				4	
8	Is hardware unavailable because the data processing function was not aware of the delivery schedule?				3	
8	Is the hardware delivery problem due to users not providing data processing with their processing requirements sufficiently in advance so that capacity could be planned?				3	
8	Is the unavailability of hardware directly due to the lack of data processing planning?				3	
9	Is the excessive computer time due to overselling on the part of the vendor?				1	
9	Is the excessive computer time due to poor planning by the data processing department?				3	
9	Is excessive computer capacity due to projected user volumes not materializing?				3	

Figure 16. Vendor problem diagnostic checklist (cont.).
(NOTE: Yes responses indicate potential computer problems.)

NO.	CAUSE OF PROBLEM		PRINCIPLE VIOLATED	RECOMMENDED SOLUTION	
	SPECIFIC	GENERAL		GENERAL	SPECIFIC
1	Vendor slow to make changes or to be available	Poor sequence	Smooth flow	Rearrange	Use competitive bidding
2	Requested changes cost extra — not included in contract	Complicated, costly	Simplicity	Improve	Establish a contract review board
3	Products not available when needed	Poor sequence	Smooth flow	Rearrange	Perform long-range EDP capacity planning
4	Products fail to work as specified	Nonessential, redundant	Productivity, need	Eliminate	Demand proof of quality for products accepted

Figure 17. Vendor problem solution matrix.

proved to be very satisfactory in the data processing field. Not unique to data processing, nevertheless they overcome the more common vendor problems occurring in contracting for services and products.

The vendor problem solutions are shown in Figure 17. The solution matrix begins by categorizing vendor problems into four causes. Note that the Figure 16 diagnostic checklist points to one of these four problem causes. The solution logic described in Figure 5 has then been applied to those problem causes to lead to specific solutions. The general solution is from Figure 5, and the specific solution is directed toward vendors. The four recommended solutions are described below:

- *Solution 1 — Use competitive bidding.* Most computer products and services are offered at a fixed price. The variable and negotiable part of most data processing contracts are the services provided in conjunction with the product ordered. For example, a payroll application may be ordered at a fixed price, but the vendor might include forty or eighty hours of on-site consulting to help install and operate the payroll application.

  Competitive bidding for data processing products and services provides the following three advantages:

  - It ensures that the major options will be evaluated (by obtaining different recommendations from different vendors)
  - It helps ensure that the lowest price for the total package will be obtained
  - It discourages vendors from becoming complacent and encourages additional services and attention

- *Solution 2 — Establish a contract review board.* Data processing contracts may require the following four categories of participants:

  - Data processing professionals
  - Users of the services being contracted for
  - Contractual expertise
  - Quality control expertise

  If any of the skills listed above are missing from the contractual negotiations, the delivered product or service may fall short of expectations. The objective in contract negotiation is to ensure that the requirements have been properly defined. If any of the parties knowledgeable in the requirements, such as quality control personnel, are excluded from the contractual negotiations, those requirements may be missing from the delivered product.

It is recommended that for each major vendor contract a contract review board be established. The objective of this review board is to challenge the completeness and specificity of the contractual requirements for each agreement. The review board should ensure that the best possible thinking has been applied to the negotiation process. It does not ensure that problems will not occur, but tends to minimize the occurrence of problems. Note that this need not be a time-consuming process. In many cases, a one-hour meeting of a review board can result in thousands of dollars of savings to the business.

- *Solution 3 — Perform long-range EDP capacity planning.* Capacity planning is designed to ensure that adequate resources will be available when needed. This planning can occur only when the following information is known:

  - New applications and workloads to be given to the data processing function
  - Expected increases in volume
  - Expected increases in size of business
  - Processing periods, such as daily or end-of-month processing
  - Hardware and software processing capacity
  - Budgetary or other business constraints

Capacity planning is a responsibility of the data processing department. The better run data processing functions prepare one- and three-year capacity plans and then update them quarterly. Note that equipment orders placed with vendors normally do not bind the business to acquire those products if 90-day cancellation notice is given.

- *Solution 4 — Demand proof of quality for products accepted.* Businesses do well to deal with quality vendors. Quality vendors can state, and then demonstrate, the expected quality of their products. Hardware products can normally be described in terms of processing capacity, uptime, and expected service costs. Software quality can be expressed in terms of software quality issues, or factors relating to data, operations, and performance. See Figure 18 for a description of these quality factors.

Those vendors who are reluctant to state quality in quantitative terms are generally not good vendors to deal with. The more general the expectations from a vendor, the more likely that the business will be disappointed with the vendor's products.

CLEANUP RULE

The best indication of performance is the success of an application, not the ballyhoo that was stated when the project was proposed.

IMPEDIMENTS TO THE CURE

There are many reasons why vendor relationships may be difficult to improve. However, even the small fish in the big pond can make some progress. Listed below are the impediments that must be considered in negotiating with vendors:

- *Little fish in a big pond.* Small companies frequently have difficulty negotiating with large vendors. This is particularly true when small businesses demand that vendors eliminate or modify a key phrase of their contractual services. Still, there are many ways of accomplishing the same objective. In dealing with large vendors, small businesses should be objective-oriented and not focus their attention on specific clauses or policies of the larger vendor.
- *It's in the contract.* Many vendors try to hold the customers to standardized contracts, claiming that is their way of doing business. This may be true, but until the deviation from the standard clause is requested, there is no way of knowing whether or not the deviation will be accepted. If it is an important consideration, the business should insist that a formal policy decision be made on the deviation before the contract is accepted or rejected.

Data Issues

During the developmental process, the quality assurance analyst should be concerned about the following data issues:

- *Accuracy/completeness* – The data entered, processed, and outputted by the application system is accurate and complete. Accuracy and completeness controls are transaction and data element oriented. Control commences when a transaction is originated and concludes when that data has been used for its intended purposes.
- *Authorization* – Data is processed in accordance with the intents of management. In an application system, there is both general and specific authorization for the processing of transactions. Control in application systems is more closely related to specific authorization to act than to general authorization.
- *File integrity* – The assurance that data entered in the application system will be returned unaltered. The file integrity procedures ensure that the right file is used and that the data on the file and the sequence in which the data is stored and retrieved is correct.
- *Reconstruction* – The ability to verify the processing of data. The propriety of data can be supported through a review trail substantiating the accuracy, completeness, and authorization of data.

Operational Issues

During the developmental process, the quality assurance analyst should be concerned about the following operational issues:

- *Continuity of processing* – The ability to sustain processing in the event problems occur. Continuity of processing assures that the necessary procedures and backup information is available to restart and recover operations should the integrity of operations be lost due to problems. Control also includes the timeliness of recovery operations and the ability to maintain processing during periods when the computer is inoperable.
- *Service levels* – Producing the desired results within a time frame acceptable to the user. Service level controls attempt to match user requirements with available resources. Processing resources include input/output capabilities, communication facilities, processing capabilities, and systems software capabilities.
- *Security* – Protecting the application system resources against accidental and intentional modification, destruction, misuse, and disclosure. Security controls are the totality of procedures ensuring the integrity of application data and programs for unintentional and unauthorized acts.
- *Cost-effectiveness* – The economics of developing, operating, and maintaining application systems. The cost-effectiveness shows the relationship between the cost to develop, cost to operate, and the benefits from operation, both tangible and intangible.

Performance Issues

During the developmental process, the quality assurance analyst should be concerned about the following performance issues.

- *Satisfaction* – The application system accomplishes the stated user objectives for the application. The objectives are the stated system requirements including maintenance requirements. The objectives should be measurable so that it can be determined definitively whether or not objectives have been achieved.
- *Compliance* – The system should be designed so that processing is in accordance with generally accepted accounting procedures, organizational policies and procedures, and governmental regulations. These requirements need to be identified, implemented, and maintained in conjunction with other requirements.

The role of the quality assurance analyst during the systems development process is to ensure that the systems development quality assurance issues are adequately addressed.

Figure 18. Quality factors[1].

[1] *Quality Assurance System Development Reviews,* copyright 1981, Quality Assurance Institute, Orlando, Fla.

- *Sales person won't process the request.* The sales person you deal with may not want to get involved in some nonstandard procedure. From the sales person's viewpoint this may be more of an annoyance than it's worth. However, from a vendor viewpoint it may be worth the annoyance. If the sales person or the service person is the stumbling block, go over his head in an attempt to obtain a favorable decision.
- *No time to negotiate.* This is frequently the killer impediment. Negotiation takes time, and data processing function or user wants the product now. The tendency is to sign the agreement and negotiate later. It just doesn't work. It's far better to take the time and negotiate the proper contract than to expend large amounts of time later trying to correct an unfavorable situation.

CLEANUP RULE
If a vendor's proposal sounds too good to be true — it's probably not true.

VENDOR PROBLEM SURVIVAL TACTICS

Two organizations combating can produce a disaster. Within an organization, there are different means of applying pressure to obtain the desired solution. When you are working with an outside party, the extra pressure may cause the vendor to walk away from a contract, making a worse mess than currently exists.

When you are caught in a vendor squeeze, the following survival tactics may help you keep the balls up in the air until a long-range solution can be developed:

1. Call for a summit meeting — The highest ranking officer in the business who is willing to get involved should meet the highest ranking vendor officer who is accessible. It is difficult for the combatants in a computer mess to arrive at a realistic solution. Senior officers who are more concerned with the survival of their business than the specific problem can negotiate from a realistic perspective. Also, these are the players who can make the on-the-spot decisions necessary to develop a compromise solution.

2. Call in the lawyers — Occasionally, a well-written letter by the business's legal counsel can work wonders. It may even be necessary to commence legal action, but in most cases it will not be necessary to conclude the legal action. This is a bluffing tactic that, although damaging to long-term relationships, can frequently accomplish a short-term objective.

3. Buy in the open market — Many products and services unobtainable from the vendor may be obtainable in the open marketplace. These open marketplace solutions include:

   — Buying hardware from a third party
   — Buying compatible hardware and software from another vendor
   — Hiring consultants to solve a problem
   — Acquiring assistance through user groups

Survival tactics are important in data processing. It is the survivors who can develop the long-range solutions. Both the survival tactic and the long-range solution should be commenced at the same time.

CLEANUP RULE

If you follow the practice of requiring vendors to demonstrate how they ensure the quality of their products, you may never have to deal with poor vendors.

5
SOLVING A CHANGING BUSINESS REQUIREMENT NEED

It is frequently said that the only thing that is constant is change. Computer systems change more than manual systems, because they are more detailed in nature. Whereas a minor change to a manual system may require only a few verbal statements, a minor change in a computer system may result in changing several hundred computer instructions.

When computer systems are first installed, the cost of development or acquisition far exceeds the cost of maintenance, i.e., change. That mix of costs gradually changes until the cost of maintenance far exceeds the cost of development. Most data processing functions now spend between two-thirds and three-fourths of their total resources on changing application systems. It is so prevalent that the name *change management* has been applied to this highly costly aspect of data processing.

The frequency and cost of change depends upon the structure of application systems and the type of business changes occurring. Data processing can do little to alter changing business conditions. These are frequently dictated by competition and regulatory agencies. Changes associated with the data processing function and the function of applications can be addressed by the data processing function.

This chapter addresses the problem of changing computerized applications. It is the major challenge in the data processing function today. The chapter provides the worksheets needed to identify the cause of problems and then offers solutions to the system change dilemma. The chapter also offers survival tactics to help when the changes cannot be made either economically or timely.

WHY IS MAINTENANCE SUCH A BIG PROBLEM?

In the early days of data processing, the U.S. Internal Revenue Service attempted to make organizations capitalize the cost of developing applications. U.S. industry banded together and won the case for expending data processing costs. While this won U.S. industry a tax advantage, it cost it the proper management perspective.

If computerized applications were capitalized, they would be considered capital assets. As such they would be managed, budgeted, and maintained as any other capital asset is. Management would not let its buildings or factories deteriorate, but, because data processing applications are expensed, management is not aware of the deterioration occurring to those assets.

Data processing systems do not deteriorate in the same manner as equipment. For example, equipment tends to wear out with use, but application software does not. If application software is properly maintained, it can exist almost indefinitely. An interesting exercise for an organization that has had the computer for a few years is to add up the total cost of acquisition and development of software packages. Some organizations conducting this exercise find out that software is their most valuable business asset.

Application software can deteriorate in any of the following manners:

- Increased rigidity — The system becomes less flexible and harder to change. Just as some products become brittle and break, so can application software, if its flexibility is not maintained through proper maintenance.
- Documentation deterioration — If the documentation is not maintained, the ability to find and correct problems increases in cost. An analogy would be an index to a filing cabinet. Once the indexing system deteriorates, users are no longer able to readily locate documents in the filing cabinet.
- Currentness with requirements — Business requirements change regardless of whether or not application software changes. When the software does not change, the processing responsibilities slowly revert to the using department. This makes the application less and less useful to the user.

The maintenance problem is that software is not recognized as a capital asset and managed as such. The problem is to allocate sufficient resources to keep the application software functioning properly. The solution is to address maintenance of software from the same perspective that management addresses maintenance of plant and office equipment.

Management should note that the deterioration of application software is widespread. Many data processing professionals accept this as normal, rather than as a significant business problem. As such, they have not alerted senior management to the problem, but many businesses find it more difficult to hide, as maintenance costs keep increasing as a percentage of total data processing costs.

SYMPTOMS OF THE CHANGING BUSINESS REQUIREMENTS PROBLEM

Information is the lifeblood of an organization. Good management decisions depend upon the currentness and correctness of information. As the integrity of the information deteriorates, so may business decisions and actions.

Maintaining the currentness of computer business applications is not a data processing challenge, it's a business necessity. Management must devise policies and plans to ensure the timely updating of its computerized application.

One major problem may be encountered in this updating policy. That is applications purchased rather than developed in-house. Some organizations use only purchased applications. In these instances, changes to those applications will depend upon the willingness of the vendor to make those changes. However, there are other ways to maintain applications than to change the program code. These solutions will be discussed later in this chapter.

The symptoms of a problem in applications maintaining currentness with business requirements are listed in Figure 19 and described in more detail below.

- *Symptom 1 – User uninformed of change.* The data processing function has many reasons to change an application system, including:
  - Improve productivity, for example, language optimizers can be purchased that improve the speed at which transactions can be processed.
  - Vendor issues new versions of operating systems, which may cause the interface parameters between the application and the operating system to be changed.

NO.	SYMPTOM	EXPLANATION	SEVERITY
1.	User uninformed of change	Data processing department changes an application system, but fails to notify the user either that the change was made or implemented.	High
2.	EDP uninformed of change	The user of the application makes a business change that impacts the application, such as additional input, but fails to notify data processing of the need to change the application.	High
3.	Manual adjustments made to computer outputs	The information contained on a computer-produced output report must be manually changed before it can be used.	High
4.	Excessive change requests to system	The user makes more change requests than data processing resources can make.	High
5.	Duplicate records maintained by user	Users keep manual records that contain the same or similar information as that contained by the computerized application.	High
6.	Over budget	The cost of making changes to an application exceeds the estimate or budget for those changes.	Medium
7.	Behind schedule	The changes requested by the user are not installed on the date the user needs them.	Medium
8.	Important projects delayed	Changes that the user needs are not installed when the user needs them, because other changes of apparent higher priority are installed first.	Medium
9.	Changes required on short notice	The user provides only minimal time between the notice to data processing that a change is needed and the date on which that change is needed.	Medium

Figure 19. Symptoms of a changing business requirements problem.

— New hardware or software requires changes to be made to an application program before the new hardware or software can be installed.

Any change to a computer application has an associated risk that that change will affect the integrity of processing. If users are notified of that change, they can prepare for and anticipate problems. When they are not notified, problems may get beyond their scrutiny, causing problems more serious than necessary.

- *Symptom 2 – EDP uninformed of change.* Users sometimes forget the impact on computer applications of changes made to their areas. For example, users may change input requirements, meaning that new product codes, etc., will be included in the input, and yet fail to notify data processing of that change. This can result in the abnormal termination of computer runs or the rejection of items or the incorrect processing of items.

The types of changes that users may make, failing to notify data processing about them, include:

— New products and other permanent information, such as prices, rates, etc.
— Expanded data fields, such as larger quantities than the field has been programmed to accept.
— Unexpected large volumes that exceed internal processing limitations.

- *Symptom 3 – Manual adjustments made to computer outputs.* Many users live with less than correct computer-produced outputs. They may not know the cause of the problem, believe they are the cause of the problem, or do not want to take the time and effort to initiate a change request. The result is that the user must manually make some change to the computer output before it can be used for its intended purpose.

The most common types of manually correctable processing includes:

— Wrong delivery location
— Incorrect master information
— Processing restriction, such as quantity limitation
— Incorrect application of processing rules

- *Symptom 4 — Excessive change requests to system.* One of the approaches used in systems design is called *prototyping.* Under this concept, a "quick-and-dirty" system is installed and then modified to meet the real requirements. The objective of this approach is to get something in quickly, so that the user can see it, and then rewrite that system to meet the real needs. Unfortunately, many prototype systems are installed that are not intended to be prototypes. This results in the user having to request major revisions to the system before it is usable.

  Systems that are subject to a high frequency of changes, for example, one or more changes per week, pose two serious problems to the business as follows:

  1. Making changes — The system is continually under change, making it difficult for the data processing department to adequately plan, implement, and test those changes.
  2. Assimilate change — When systems change too fast, it is difficult for the clerical people using those systems to assimilate those changes into their day-to-day procedures.

- *Symptom 5 — Duplicate records maintained by user.* Some users maintain duplicate sets of records. One set is maintained by the computer, and another is manually maintained by the user. These redundant records pose two problems to the business. First is the excessive cost of maintaining two sets of records, and second is which set of records should the user rely upon. The reliance answer is usually the records maintained by the user.

  Duplicate records are maintained by users for any of the following reasons:

  - The computer application is prone to error.
  - The user does not understand the computer and thus does not believe computer processing is trustworthy.
  - The user maintains duplicate records as a means of controlling the computer system.

- *Symptom 6 — Over budget.* The cost of budgeting changes is usually different from the cost of budgeting new systems. Changes are normally small, and thus the cost seems insignificant. Because these costs rarely have to be justified, they are considered a cost of doing business, and they are not subject to the same managerial control as requests to acquire new applications.

The over-budget symptom is frequently associated with the rathole theory. The rathole theory says that past costs are ignored and only current and future costs are considered. Therefore anything that has been spent is considered to be thrown down the rathole. When a maintenance change is requested, the managerial decision is: Should we continue the system and pay for that change or acquire a new costly system? Using this theory, the change is almost always approved. It is this same theory that stops us from trading in old junker automobiles, even though we spend more money to maintain those cars than the payments for a new automobile.

- *Symptom 7 — Behind schedule.* The reason maintenance falls behind schedule is different from the reasons for the acquisition of new products to fall behind schedule. The predominating reason maintenance is behind schedule is because maintenance tends to be an unplanned part of the data processing function. New computer systems used to be months and even years behind schedule until managerial planning was brought to bear on the developmental process. Maintenance changes will probably be behind schedule until those same managerial processes are used for maintenance.
- *Symptom 8 — Important projects delayed.* A large number of maintenance changes makes it necessary for data processing to allocate resources among those changes. Some can be installed immediately, while others are delayed. Most data processing groups allocate resources based on application, and not business needs. Therefore, one application can have all of its changes installed, while another is heavily backlogged. In this type of environment, the squeaky wheel gets the oil, meaning that low-priority business changes may be installed ahead of high-priority business changes.
- *Symptom 9 — Changes required on short notice.* One of the challenges of the data processing profession is to get changes in quickly. It's not uncommon for a user to dump change requests on the data processing manager Friday afternoon and want them in Monday morning. In some instances, these time

spans cannot be controlled by the user, but in other instances users sit on the changes for days or weeks and then demand extraordinary efforts on the part of the data processing staff to get the changes in when the user requests them. In other instances, users request the changes before they need them, so that if they are not installed on time the users have a buffer area in which to put extra pressure. Though this practice may be good for the user, it may be bad for the business.

CHANGING BUSINESS REQUIREMENTS
PROBLEM DIAGNOSTIC CHECKLIST

The diagnostic checklist is the tool of the auditor and consultant. These individuals accumulate through experience the most probable items to go wrong. They then incorporate these items into a check-list. Through the use of these checklists, auditors and consultants are able to transfer the experience of the more senior people to the junior people. This same principle has been incorporated into the diagnostic checklists included in this book.

The diagnostic checklists throughout this book are designed so that yes responses indicate good data processing practices and no responses represent potential problem areas. These checklists, unlike the auditor and consultant checklists, are symptom-driven. This means that the identified symptom, those described in Figure 19 for changing business requirements problems, are the starting point in a diagnostic checklist. Those items for which a yes response is provided point to the most probable cause and solution for that problem (see Solution Ref. No. column, which points to the solution matrix presented in Figure 21). The diagnostic checklist for changing business requirement problems (see Figure 20) is designed to be used by senior management. Because many of the problems are beyond the solution of the data processing manager, the involvement of senior management is normally essential to ensure the acceptance of a workable solution.

CLEANUP RULE
Anything that works should never be changed.

SYMPTOM NO.	ITEM	RESPONSE			SOLUTION REF. NO.	COMMENTS
		YES	NO	NA		
1	Did DP fail to notify the user of a change because it felt the change did not directly affect the user (for example, it was associated with an operating system change)?				5	
1	Was the user uninformed because there was no formal method for communicating changes to the user?				5	
1	Was the user informed of a change, but did not recognize that the item being discussed was a change to the system?				3	
2	Did the user fail to notify DP of the change because of a lack of a formal change process?				5	
2	Did the user fail to recognize the need to inform EDP of the change?				5	
2	Did the user inform EDP of the change, but fail to indicate what type of change was needed to the automated application?				3	
3	Are manual adjustments made because the computer system produced erroneous results?				3	
3	Are manual adjustments made to computer output because the user does not want to pay to change the application?				4	
3	Are manual adjustments made to computer output because the user does not know how to request computer changes?				5	
4	Are excess change requests submitted by the user because the system is inadequate to meet the user's real needs?				3	
4	Are excess change requests made because the user wants a new application system?				1 3	
4	Are excessive change requests made because the user does not understand how to use the system?				6	
5	Does the user maintain duplicate records because he doesn't understand the system?				6	

Figure 20. Changing business requirements problem diagnostic checklist.
(Note: Yes responses indicate potential computer problems.)

SYMPTOM NO.	ITEM	RESPONSE			SOLUTION REF. NO.	COMMENTS
		YES	NO	NA		
5	Does the user maintain duplicate records because the system fails to meet the user's needs?				3	
5	Does the user maintain duplicate records because he does not feel the system is adequately controlled?				5	
6	Is the application over budget because changes to purchased applications are too costly?				1	
6	Is the project over budget because proposed or installed changes are costly?				4	
7	Are the changes behind schedule because they take too long to install?				5	
7	Are changes behind schedule because they have been bumped by high priority changes?				2	
7	Are changes to purchased applications behind schedule because of the high cost of making the change?				1	
8	Are projects delayed because higher priority projects bump them?				2	
8	Are changes to application systems delayed because data processing doesn't fully understand the change requests?				5	
8	Are changes delayed because of the high estimates to install those changes?				1 4	
9	Are changes requested on short notice made because the user doesn't understand the system?				6	
9	Are changes requested on short notice because of the lack of a formal change request system?				5	
9	Are changes requested on short notice because they were given the wrong priority initially?				2	

Figure 20. Changing business requirements problem diagnostic checklist (cont.).
(Note: Yes responses indicate potential computer problems.)

SOLUTIONS TO CHANGING BUSINESS REQUIREMENTS PROBLEMS

Management is paid for solutions, not problems. Solutions to technical problems always appear harder than solutions to nontechnical problems. This is frequently because the technical problems stay in the bottom of the in basket and fester, rather than being quickly addressed before they become serious.

The problem-solving steps, if properly performed, lead the user to the solution to that problem. The solutions to problems associated with changing business requirements are presented in Figure 21. This matrix shows the most probable causes of changing requirements problems and then leads the reader through the problem-solving methodology presented in Figure 5 to a general and specific solution.

These solutions listed in Figure 21 work in practice. The implementation and description of the six changing requirement solutions follow:

- *Solution 1 – Develop pre- and postprocessors.* Purchased application systems can be maintained in one of two ways. First, the vendor can be contacted and a change requested. If approved by the vendor, the change will be implemented and provided to the organization. If the change is a permanent change to the application, it will be carried forward to future applications. If this is a special change, however, it will have to be rerequested each time the vendor issues a new version of the software. In addition, the business may have to pay to have the change implemented.

  The second method of changing a purchased application is to develop a preprocessor, a postprocessor, or both. This means that a program is written that does some processing before the transaction is entered into the purchased application or performs processing after the purchased application has completed processing or both. For example, if a purchased application permits only a price up to $99.99 and a product for over $100 is acquired, then a postprocessor can identify that product and change the price after the purchased application has completed invoicing. These alternative processing solutions may be much less in cost and quicker to implement than requests made to the application vendor.

NO.	CAUSE OF PROBLEM		PRINCIPLE VIOLATED	RECOMMENDED SOLUTION	
	SPECIFIC	GENERAL		GENERAL	SPECIFIC
1	Purchased application cannot (economically) be modified as needed	Inconvenient location	Smooth flow	Rearrange	Develop pre- and post-processors
2	Changes take too long to install	Poor sequence	Smooth flow	Rearrange	Establish a change priority system
3	System performs as specified, but fails to satisfy user's needs	Nonessential, redundant	Productivity, need	Eliminate	Establish critical success factors
4	Desired changes are too costly	Complicated, costly	Simplicity	Improve	Study alternative processing modes
5	Lack of communication between users and DP	Nonessential, redundant	Productivity, need	Eliminate	Establish a system change form
6	User doesn't know how to use system	Fragmented, improper skills	Productivity, flow	Change, combine	Develop a user manual

Figure 21. Changing business requirements problem solution matrix.

- *Solution 2 — Establish a change priority system.* Changes should not be put in at the discretion of the data processing project personnel. A prioritization system should be established under the control of the user or users. Two types of priority systems can be established. The first is an application/user priority system in which the user establishes priorities. In such a system, the algorithm is relatively simple, such as a sequential priority with priority 1 installed before priority 2, which is installed before priority 3, etc., or a high, medium, low prioritization system. The second method is a business-oriented prioritization method, in which senior management establishes the prioritization system and then users classify the change within that system. The type of business priorities that can be used include:

  - Competitive advantage
  - Cost reduction
  - Legislative requirement
  - Data processing operational change
  - More extensive information
  - Convenience of user (such as correcting the spelling of a name or clarifying the title of a report)
  - Reduce losses due to such things as incorrectly priced product
  - Reduce fraud and embezzlement

- *Solution 3 — Establish critical success factors.* Critical success factors are the criteria by which the success of an application system will be judged. If changes are made to the application system, these are the criteria by which the successful implementation of the change will be judged. If the user must state the evaluation criteria, the data processing department has a much higher probability of satisfying the user requirements. The success criteria should be considered an integral part of the change request. The change request form asks the user to state both the change requested and then the criteria by which the successful implementation of that change will be judged.

- *Solution 4 — Study alternative processing modes.* Many users request a change to their application system. The data processing department comes back with the specifications and cost of that change. It is viewed as a take-it-or-leave-it situation. The user can accept the change or reject the change. Many users do not consider requesting alternative solutions. Depending on the completeness of the requirements, the proposed solution may be a systems analyst's interpretation of what the user wanted. With additional amplification and clarification, an alternative solution may be proposed at a much lower cost. In addition, the data processing department may have proposed a Cadillac solution for a Chevrolet problem.

- *Solution 5 — Establish a system change form.* The point at which a user requests change is a critical communication point. Users are attempting to describe what must be changed in an application system to accomplish a business objective. The less formally this change request is stated, the higher the probability that it will be incorrectly implemented. The solution is to formalize the change request and the information included on that request form. At a minimum, the change request form should include:

  - System name
  - Objective of change
  - Data affected by change
  - Detailed description of change
  - Priority of change
  - Impediments to change, if any
  - Impact on business if change is not installed within one day, one week, and one month

- *Solution 6 — Develop a user manual.* Application systems can be used properly only when the user knows how to use them. Think for a moment about some relatively complex technical tool, such as a pocket calculator, that you own. Now think which features on that pocket calculator you use and which you don't use. Odds are that you use a subset of the total features, because that is what you have learned. Likewise, in computer applications users use those processing features they understand; they don't use those they don't understand. A user manual increases the probability that users will understand how to use the full features of the application designed to assist them in their jobs.

IMPEDIMENTS TO THE PROPOSED CHANGING REQUIREMENT SOLUTIONS

The key to developing an effective change process is to formalize it. This runs counter to two basic human problems. The first is resistance to change, and the second is resistance to formality.

Data processing professionals are frequently referred to as *change makers*. When people initiate change, they must also initiate the procedures to help sell that change to the effective parties. These marketing efforts for change must overcome the following impediments:

- *Willingness to let change system be circumvented.* Close working relationships and favored users result in accepting and implementing undocumented, unprioritized changes. Unless senior management is willing to back data processing management in enforcing the change system, it can break down quickly, particularly in small organizations.
- *Management permits the structure of applications to deteriorate.* Inadequate managerial attention and resources will be applied to maintaining the structure of the application system. With purchased applications, new enhancements and maintenance contracts might not be acquired, and with in-house-developed applications the structure may not be kept current with technological changes.
- *The squeaky wheel gets the oil.* An orderly structure can be maintained only when a preplanned prioritization system is utilized. If management permits those priority systems to be regularly overridden without strong cause, other than the personal demands of the manager, the change method begins to slowly deteriorate.

Few organizations are able to develop companywide approaches to maintenance. Most organizations have strong users, who tend to dominate data processing and consume an excessive amount of data processing resources. These practices tend to continue until senior management of the organization treats data as a resource of the organization and manages it as such.

CHANGING REQUIREMENTS SURVIVAL TACTICS

Most application systems cannot be stopped until they can be adequately repaired or enhanced. Unless processing can be continued, losses may accrue to the organization. Some of the survival tactics that can be used until application systems can be changed include:

1. Eliminate troublesome transactions — If a particular transaction is causing problems, it can be eliminated from processing. For example, if the sale of a particular product causes the system to abnormally terminate, then that transaction can be eliminated and the remaining transactions processed.
2. Perform processing manually — If a vendor of a purchased application, or an in-house-developed application, cannot be changed by the time a new requirement must be operational, those new processing requirements can be performed manually. In many instances, this may require overtime or managerial involvement because of the complexity of processing, but it can avoid missing a scheduled deadline.
3. Delay implementing the requirement — Painful as it may seem to management, few businesses fail because a specific requirement is not implemented on the scheduled date. Management must carefully weigh the impact on the organization and its position in the marketplace. If the risk of installing it is greater than the risk of not installing it, the requirements should be delayed.

It is important that the appropriate level of management be involved in selecting a survival tactic. If the survival measure affects only a single department, that department manager can make the survival decision, but if the requirement affects two or more departments, the survival tactic should be selected by senior management.

CLEANUP RULE
It is far simpler to request a change to a computer application than to implement it. Any help the requester can provide the implementer should be provided.

6
SOLVING A MISUSE OF THE SYSTEM PROBLEM

Most feel that it is people who are intimidated and abused by computers. One must recognize that computers also take abuse from people. It would be reasonable to start a group whose purpose is "the prevention of cruelty to computers by people."

Computers are machines, and systems are predefined methods of accomplishing work. We recognize that machines can be abused, and if they are, they may fail more frequently or cease performing. Likewise, systems whose users fail to follow the rules may produce inaccurate results or terminate processing. If everyone did his job correctly, there would be very few problems with data processing systems. Unfortunately, people are human and unpredictable and therefore have abused, are abusing, and will continue to abuse computer systems.

This chapter addresses the problem of misuse of computer systems by users. For at least one chapter, the data processing function will be excused as the cause of the problem. However, this does not mean that it cannot contribute to the solution.

The chapter explains where the problems occur in the developmental life cycle and then how to identify and diagnose the problems associated with system misuse. Some immediately implementable solutions are proposed for this problem area, together with suggestions on how to survive until those solutions can be effected.

THE CAUSES OF USER DATA PROBLEMS

The U.S. General Accounting Office (GAO), an investigative arm of the U.S. Congress, conducts reviews of federal computer systems. After many years of conducting reviews, the General Accounting Office summarized the problems it uncovered in federal systems. The problems were divided into software problems (programming problems) and data problems. The cause of programming problems will

be discussed in Chapter 7. The data problems are primarily attributable to user abuse of computer systems.

The GAO categorized data problems into the following six areas:

1. *Forms designed and used for input preparation are too complex.* Systems are frequently designed by engineers with a
   doctorate degree for clerks with a high-school education who
   are performing relatively routine and sometimes boring jobs.
   Filling out complex forms correctly may be a greater challenge
   than these clerks are equal to. As a result, data is entered
   incorrectly, incorrectly entered in the wrong columns, or not
   entered at all.

   Data processing professionals call this concept garbage in,
   garbage out (GIGO). Users believing in the infallibility of the
   computer also call it GIGO, but their definition of that
   acronym is garbage in, gospel out. Users do not understand
   the impact of entering bad data on the integrity of processing
   of computer systems.

   Complex input forms used for data entry purposes lead
   to other problems. Data entry operators need to create a
   certain rhythm if they are to reduce error. The same analogy
   holds true for a golf or tennis swing. If a player slows or
   speeds up the swing, the result is a much poorer shot in most
   cases. Complex forms tend to cause data entry errors.

2. *EDP files are not always adequately reviewed to assure that
   good data is being used.* Computer files are a large, complex
   organization of data. In many instances, it is difficult to get
   data from a computer file in an easy-to-read and use format.
   For this reason, the individuals responsible for data on the
   computer file may never look at the data. In manual files it is
   possible to browse through the records and spot unusual items.
   The same unusual items in a computer file may go unnoticed,
   because those records are not reviewed. For example, charges
   in an accounts receivable file that cannot be associated with
   any customer may be stored in a suspense account (a holding
   account for unmatched data) for long periods of time and
   eventually may have to be written off as uncollectible.

3. *Instructions to people preparing data input are not always
   provided, are provided late, or are not adequate.* The people

in the trenches of data input preparation are sometimes the forgotten people. Because they are on the periphery of the computer system, they are not involved in mainstream activities. The instructions they are provided are frequently minimal and may be given only once. As people turn over and are replaced, the new people receive only that subset of information known and remembered by the individual being replaced. After two or three replacements the instructions become sketchier and sketchier.

Many data processing system designers believe that input preparation is intuitively obvious. They are intricately familiar with the system, which makes input preparation seem simple. Unfortunately, those charged to perform the input preparation may not understand the system, do not understand the transaction they are preparing, and may not know whether they are entering it correctly or incorrectly — and in addition, they may not care.

4. *Preparers of input data are not always adequately trained.* Instructions to people preparing input and training are closely related. The instructions tell what to do, the training tells how to do it. As systems change, new instructions may be prepared, but people are not trained in how to use those instructions. Murphy has stated that "what can go wrong will go wrong," and he is proved right thousands of times per day. Management should not hold untrained people responsible for incorrect acts. Proper training is a management responsibility.

5. *Manual reviews of input documents are not always adequate.* Once prepared, input documents are rarely reviewed. Even supervisory approval is frequently a cursory process resulting in little more than adding the supervisor's initials to a document. People without instructions and training are very likely to make errors and not know it. Unless those documents are reviewed, the errors will be entered into the computer system.

6. *High volumes of transaction cause input preparers to make errors (workload pressures).* The major variable in computer workload is input preparation. Increased volume has minimal effect on processing time. Once people get overloaded, their

error rate tends to increase. Because most systems operate in a secular format, workloads vary from day to day and hour to hour, with high workload periods causing more input errors.

CLEANUP RULE

To make mistakes in processing is human, but to really foul up you need to enter erroneous input into a computer system.

SYMPTOMS OF THE MISUSE OF THE SYSTEM PROBLEM

System abuse is a new disease in the annals of business. It parallels the age-old rivalry between accountants and marketing personnel regarding the selling price of a product. Accountants want to make profit, and marketing people want to move product. In computer abuse, the users state that the problem is a system problem, and systems people state that it is a user problem.

Some people describe a computer system as an accident waiting to happen. It is embedded with a series of potential time bombs ready to explode into system problems at any point in time. The key for management is to identify and defuse these problems before they become serious.

The symptoms associated with a misuse of the system problem are listed in Figure 22, together with the severity of that symptom, and described below:

- *Symptom 1 — Inability of staff to diagnose cause of problem.* The means of uncovering an error or notifying a user of a system error vary based on the system design, but generally fall into one of the following categories:

  1. System error message — An indication that a system rule has been violated.
  2. System warning message — An indication that there may be a potential problem, for example, the quantity of product ordered may be out of line with typical orders.

NO.	SYMPTOM	EXPLANATION	SEVERITY
1.	Inability of staff to diagnose cause of problem	The user of the system encounters a problem, but cannot determine the cause of the problem	High
2.	Input data lost	The user enters data into the computer system, but that data either never arrives or is lost during processing or output	High
3.	Unassigned responsibility	Some aspect of user responsibility is unassigned to a specific individual for completion and control	High
4.	No one accepts responsibility for a problem	A problem in the computer system occurs for which no one accepts responsibility, thus delaying the corrective process	High
5.	Customer complaint	A third-party customer (neither data processing nor the user of the system) is unhappy with some aspect of the system; for example, a customer believes he is incorrectly invoiced	High
6.	System abuse for personal gain	Some member of the organization uses the system resources to gain some personal advantage, such as fraud, operating a service bureau on the company's computer, or sabotage to make someone or the company look bad	High
7.	Input data wrong	The data entered into the computer system is erroneous	Medium
8.	User complaint	The user of the computer system is unhappy with the service or processing results produced by the system	Medium
9.	System abuse — unintentional	Due to improper use of the computer system, the integrity of a transaction or processing is lost	Medium

Figure 22. Symptoms of a misuse of the system problem.

3. Processing result appears to be erroneous to users based on their experience and knowledge of the system.
4. Data or transaction is missing from computer outputs.
5. Control totals are out of balance.
6. Data is garbled.

Once the problem is recognized, the person uncovering the problem should be able to diagnose the cause and make the correction. In many cases, the user has neither sufficient information nor sufficient knowledge, training, or experience to perform the diagnosis and take the appropriate corrective action. In some instances, the wrong corrective action will be taken, or no corrective action will be taken. Frequently, a committee of users and data processing personnel will have to be assembled to uncover the cause and correct the problem.

- *Symptom 2 — Input data lost.* Data received by the user for entry into the computer system may not be processed. The reasons that data might be lost include:

  - Loss of physical input source document prior to entry into the computer
  - Miscoded and rejected from processing, with the rejected message lost
  - Equipment failure, such as messages lost due to hardware failure at central processing site
  - Processing error in computer system
  - Actually processed, but processing not recognized

- *Symptom 3 — Unassigned responsibility.* As job functions are computerized, responsibilities change. In many instances, responsibilities are transferred from the user department to the data processing department or other function, such as a data base administrator (an individual whose responsibility is to control the use of data in the organization). Just because one person gives up a responsibility does not mean that it is accepted and performed by another. In designing the system, management should make an inventory of job responsibilities and then ensure, after the computer system is operational, that those responsibilities have been properly reassigned.

- *Symptom 4 — No one accepts responsibility for a problem.* This should be a familiar system for senior management. Something goes wrong in an application system and the finger pointing begins. Sometimes it is a two-way street, with the user pointing to the data processor, and the data processor pointing to the user. If the systems are more complex with multiple users, we can visualize a circle of people all pointing to each other.

The net result of such a situation may be a slow, corrective process. Rather than addressing the problem, people begin building "alibi files" supporting their contention that the problem is not their fault. The more serious the problem, the more finger pointing is likely to occur. The solution, of course, is to have well-defined error correction responsibilities.

- *Symptom 5 – Customer complaint.* Many organizations receive letters from their customers with the salutation "Dear Computer." These are letters of customers who have become frustrated by the business's computer system and don't know how to solve the problem. A classic story in data processing is the customer who received an invoice for $00.00. The customer, pleased that no funds were owed, threw out the notice. A month later, the same customer received an overdue notice for the same amount, requesting immediate payment or the customer's credit would be impaired. Thinking it a joke, the customer again threw it out, until the 60-day notice arrived, assessing interest and penalty charges of $00.00 and threatening law suits unless the amount was paid immediately. Completely frustrated, the customer wrote out a check to the company for $00.00 and promptly received a letter from the business's computer thanking the customer for the payment and encouraging the customer to do more business with the organization.

  Customer complaints should be monitored closely. Frequently, internal problems are hidden, but customer complaints cannot be hidden. Just as the president of the United States keeps tabs on the frequency and types of correspondence received, so should senior management keep the same type of information on computer-related complaints from their customers.

- *Symptom 6 – System abuse for personal gain.* Computer crime and abuse have been accelerating rapidly during the last decade. These differ from traditional crime in that they are usually performed by highly respected people in the organization. In addition, the dollars associated per computer crime are normally higher than the dollars associated with noncomputer crime. Most of the problems originate with falsifying input, adding to it, or deleting from it in the computer system.

Many of the acts and, according to an IBM study, the majority of computer abuses are carried out by disgruntled employees. These computer abuses are not designed for financial gain, but rather to get even with an individual or the company or just to prove that the employee beat the computer system. Many employees today have spent years playing computer games and look at beating a business's computer as another game.

The criteria associated with abuses of this type are frequently indistinguishable from everyday problems and can include:

- System abnormal termination
- Hardware damage
- Out-of-balance conditions
- Transactions missing
- Products shipped to nonexistent customers at hold areas, such as airports, and then lost

- *Symptom 7 – Input data wrong.* The data sent to the computer system fails to meet the processing rules of the system. These erroneous transactions can be rejected for reentry or may be processed through the system, producing incorrect processing results.
- *Symptom 8 – User complaints.* Users are the individuals responsible for the accuracy, completeness, timeliness, and authorization of transactions processed by the computer system. Their reaction to problems can result in a change request to the system or in lodging a complaint against the data processing department. When good working relationships exist, problems are usually handled through change request procedures. Where strained relations exist, problems are usually brought to the attention of management through user complaints. Note that even if the cause of a problem appears to be with the user, such as incorrectly entered input, the user may complain about the system's inability to handle that incorrect transaction properly.
- *Symptom 9 – System abuse – unintentional.* Murphy speaks eloquently about the initiation of problems. In most cases, the

problems associated with computer systems are caused unintentionally through ignorance on the part of the user. Most computer systems are complex and have extensive and detailed instructions on how to use the system properly. If those instructions are not followed properly, the system results may be incorrectly reported. As can be seen by the GAO study of data-related problems, the lack of instructions and training leads to the unintentional initiation of problems into computer systems.

CLEANUP RULE

Whenever management is attempting to decide whether the cause of a problem is related to greed or incompetence, incompetence should win every time.

MISUSE OF SYSTEM DIAGNOSTIC CHECKLIST

One of management's diagnostic problems is determining who is providing the correct input. Parties involved in a computer mess tend to provide answers to questions that are favorable to their position and unfavorable to the other party's position. Answers to management's questions also tend to minimize the severity of the problem unless there is a rivalry between two or more departments, causing one party to have a reason to cause problems for the other party.

Investigators have found a solution to determining who is providing the correct responses to questions. Some call this the *Colombo technique.* Colombo, as you probably are aware, was a television detective. The technique used by Colombo was to ask the potential suspect questions to which Colombo knew the answer. These are referred to as *Colombo questions.* During the investigation, Colombo would always gather some unfavorable information about a suspect and then question the suspect about it. If a suspect answered the question properly, in other words tended to incriminate himself to provide the correct response, Colombo could rely upon that individual and his response. If the respondent's answer was incorrect or if the respondent hedged, however, then Colombo knew that that individual was probably the guilty party. This is a very powerful investigative technique and should be incorporated into some of the probing performed by management into a computer mess.

To assist in developing questions to ask, Figure 23 provides diagnostic questions for analyzing the misuse of a computer system. These questions are directly related to the symptoms listed in Figure 22. Yes responses to the listed items indicate that the symptoms should be investigated further. The number in the solution reference column refers to both the probable cause associated with that symptom and the proposed solution to the problem (see Figure 24).

As previously stated, the items on the diagnostic checklist are items to be answered by the person using the checklist. It normally requires some investigation and probing for management to be able to answer the items. It is suggested that Colombo questions be incorporated in the probing to validate the correctness of the responses from the involved parties.

MISUSE OF THE SYSTEM PROBLEM SOLUTIONS

Computer systems have had problems since the first computer system went operational. In many instances, these problems were directly associated with user misuse of the system. Some organizations require that industrial psychologists be involved in the system development process to help minimize user antagonism toward the computer and reduce the human factors affecting system problems.

The introduction of the computer system into a user department has three negative effects associated with it. First is the previously discussed resistance to change. Second, the computer is a threat that may lead to the elimination of jobs. Third, computer systems may be dehumanizing, reducing an interesting job function to one that is repetitious, nonchallenging, and boring.

The industrial psychologists' solution to many of the user problems was heavy user involvement in the system design and maintenance process. This is a golden rule of data processing. It is not listed as a specific solution, because it is the lack of user involvement that leads to a computer mess. Unfortunately, if the system is developed without user involvement, one cannot go back and redo the system with user involvement.

SYMPTOM NO.	ITEM	RESPONSE			SOLUTION REF. NO.	COMMENTS
		YES	NO	NA		
1	Is the inability of the user to diagnose system problems due to the user's lack of knowledge about the system?				4	
1	Is the user's inability to diagnose a problem due to a lack of understanding about the reason for diagnostic messages?				5	
1	Is the user's inability to diagnose a problem due to ignorance of how to begin the corrective process?				2	
2	Is input lost in the user area?				1	
2	Is input lost in the movement of input from the user to the data processing area?				3	
2	Is input lost during computer processing?				3	
3	Are there unassigned responsibilities in input preparation?				1	
3	Are there unassigned responsibilities in the use of computer output?				5	
3	Are there unassigned responsibilities in the control of computer processing?				3	
4	Has the DP department failed to develop a diagnostic process for computer problems?				2	
4	Is it difficult to define the individual responsible for the control of each data item in the system?				3	
4	Are the individuals assigned systems responsibility untrained in how to fulfill those responsibilities?				4	
5	Is it difficult to determine the frequency and type of user complaints?				3	
5	Are users and data processing personnel regularly uninformed about how to avoid the situations that led to customer complaints?				4	
5	Are customers of the system unaware of who to contact regarding computer system complaints?				3	

Figure 23. Misuse of the system problem diagnostic checklist.
(NOTE: Yes responses are indicative of potential computer problems.)

SYMPTOM NO.	ITEM	RESPONSE			SOLUTION REF. NO.	COMMENTS
		YES	NO	NA		
6	Are employees involved with computer systems hired without a background check being performed?				3	
6	Are system controls inadequate to detect computer abuse problems?				3	
6	Can authorized individuals access the system to perform work-related tasks, because adequate access controls have not been established?				3	
7	Is input data entered incorrectly because the process is too complex?				1	
7	Is data entered incorrectly because the users do not understand the system rules?				4	
7	Is management unaware of the frequency and type of data input errors occurring, so that it cannot take appropriate corrective action?				3	
8	Are users unable to record and forward complaints to the data processing area due to the lack of a formal process?				3	
8	Are user complaints made because users don't understand how to recover from a user-initiated problem?				2	
8	Are user complaints ignored by the data processing function?				3	
9	Does the system fail to record, summarize, and present defects to management regularly?				3	
9	Is management unaware of the habitual error makers and how those errors affect the proper performance of their jobs?				4	
9	Does management fail to take action to remove individuals who make continuous errors and yet cannot improve their system performance?				3	

Figure 23. Misuse of the system problem diagnostic checklist (cont.).
(NOTE: Yes responses are indicative of potential computer problems.)

NO.	CAUSE OF PROBLEM		PRINCIPLE VIOLATED	RECOMMENDED SOLUTION	
	SPECIFIC	GENERAL		GENERAL	SPECIFIC
1	System input requirements are not known	Complicated, costly	Simplicity	Improve	Develop input forms and screens with user instructions
2	User doesn't know how to get out of a problem	Complicated, costly	Simplicity	Improve	Create help routines and messages
3	Controls in system are not adequate to detect or prevent certain types of misuses	Noncompliance, ineffective	Compliance	Comply, revise	Develop integrity controls
4	Lack of skills in using the system	Complicated, costly	Simplicity	Improve	Conduct training for users
5	User does not know how to utilize or interpret output features	Complicated, costly	Simplicity	Improve	Prepare guide for output usage

Figure 24. Misuse of the system problem solution matrix.

CLEANUP RULE

You can't build quality into a system after the fact. Heavy user involvement in systems design and maintenance is the key to ensuring that a quality system is built the first time.

The solutions that do work in cleaning up a computer mess associated with misuse of the system by the user include:

- *Solution 1 — Develop input forms and screens with user instructions.* Users need formal ways to interface with the computer system. This is best accomplished with easy-to-use forms or screens (a screen is the equivalent of a form displayed on a computer terminal). Detailed instructions should then be prepared on how to use each form or screen. The best instructions pictorially represent the form or screen and then number each user-entered piece of data on that form or screen. The instructions then explain what the user must do to enter the data correctly.
- *Solution 2 — Create help routines and messages.* If there is a flaw in a computer system, people will find it quickly. In the average computer system, there are literally millions of different processing variations. It is neither possible nor practical for the developer of the system to have properly identified each of those million or so processing variations, included the proper instructions for processing each variation, and then adequately tested each one to ensure that it works. What the developer can do is provide a series of aids to help users of the system get out of trouble should they get into trouble. For example, if the system is not designed to accept a certain type of terminal action, the system should explain in detail why that action is not workable and what alternatives the user has. Messages such as "command invalid" don't provide the type of help that the user needs. Good on-line systems design includes a routine called *help*. If the user types in that message, the system goes into a routine to help the user overcome a processing problem. In batch systems, computer messages provide the same type of assistance.

- *Solution 3 — Develop integrity controls.* Controls are designed to reduce the risks inherent in computer systems. Controls cannot be adequately designed and implemented until the risks are known. Management should be aware that no computer science curriculum in any college or university teaches computer science majors how to design controls. Therefore, few computer systems have formally identified the risks and then designed systems of controls specifically oriented to reduce those risks.

  Management should determine first that the major computer risks have been identified, and second that either manual or automated controls have been developed to reduce the more significant risks. If the risks have not been identified, management should insist that an exercise be undertaken.

- *Solution 4 — Conduct training for users.* Dr. W. Edward Deming, architect of the recovery of the Japanese industry, has stated that massive training is an integral part of quality work. Dr. Deming recommended that all employees should undergo formal training in how to perform their job functions. They should then be evaluated and tested on their mastery of their job assignment. Supervision should work with them up to the point that they have fully mastered their job responsibilities. At that point, they should be expected to perform flawlessly. If an individual, after being thoroughly trained and tested, cannot perform the job properly, he should be replaced.

- *Solution 5 — Prepare guide for output usage.* The user's involvement with computer systems is primarily in the input and output areas. It is as important to explain how to use output as it is to explain how to prepare input. Many of the tools and aids provided by computer systems are not utilized because the users don't understand the intent behind issuing that type of information. A story is told of one clerk using certain reports as a means of elevating himself on his chair, rather than for the intended purpose. Because the clerk didn't know what the reports were for, he made sure, at least, that they didn't go to waste.

  The same type of document should be prepared for output reports as input. A sample report should be shown. Each data item should be circled and numbered. An explanation should then be provided on the purpose and objective of each item included on an output report.

CLEANUP RULE
What the user doesn't know can hurt the business. Training is not a luxury in the computer field — it's a necessity.

IMPEDIMENTS TO SOLVING SYSTEM MISUSE PROBLEMS

In many businesses, the users do not feel that the computer system is theirs. It belongs to the data processing department. Therefore, problems belong to the data processing department, and not them. When one does not have problems, one has no need to correct them.

The specific impediments that cause difficulty in correcting user misuse of automated applications include:

- *Training is a vacation not a necessity.* It is highly probable that an input preparer or output user of a data processing application should spend two or more weeks in training to use that system correctly. Many managers do not believe they can afford this expense. In more complex systems it may take a month or more of training to fully qualify an individual to do a job. This is what Dr. Deming says is essential. Contrast this to the sink-or-swim attitude of many supervisors, and the reason for computer messes becomes more obvious.
- *Poorly designed systems.* Systems with defective design tend to cause more problems than they correct. Frequently we blame people for causing errors, when in fact it is the system that causes errors. In a previous example, we discussed how a data entry operator may make more errors when the input format is improperly designed. Many times management wants to treat symptoms rather than causes of problems. This symptom-treating impediment continues to mask the real problem.
- *It's not a serious problem.* The severity of many computer problems is not known. The system does not have the ability to provide adequate diagnosis, and therefore when solutions are

proposed they are put aside as unnecessary. This is frequently because the problems are not recorded and tabulated. Donn Parker, noted computer abuse expert, has stated on many occasions that each computer crime he has investigated has had a complete trail describing the crime, who did it, and the magnitude of the crime. In most cases, the messages were considered to be routine and never addressed in light of the actual severity of the problem.

SYSTEM MISUSE SURVIVAL TACTICS

Life is a continual battle. Problems are not the exception but rather the rule. Users who do not consider survival tactics are not dealing with real-world computer environments.

Computer misuse is one of the more common problems in computer systems today. The studies by the U.S. General Accounting Office support the thesis that improperly entered data is the major cause of computer problems. The survival tactics that can be used in this problem area include:

1. Back out and reenter — Computer transactions that pose system problems should be deleted from the system and reentered. In many instances, the system itself will delete these improper transactions with a message indicating the unacceptability and the reason for unacceptability. In other instances, a deletion process will have to be used to remove the incorrect record and reenter the transaction correctly.
2. Manually correct output — Sometimes it is easier to manually correct the situation than to attempt to do it on the computer. Though this is admitting defeat, it may be the economical and practical way to solve a problem. Some of the ways that transactions can be manually adjusted include:
   - Issue a credit or other manual adjustment to put the computer system in balance and then make a manual adjustment to the customer's records
   - Delete the transaction from the computer system and process it entirely manually
   - Break a single transaction up into multiple transactions if the individual pieces can be processed correctly

3. Replace the coach — In some instances, the problem is people. It is either an attitude problem, a skill problem, or a personality problem. It may be easier to transfer or fire an individual than to attempt to retrain and resolve disputes. This is particularly true when the same individual causes the same type of problems repetitively.

CLEANUP RULE
A computer system does what you tell it to do, not what you want it to do. Following the system rules is essential if correct results are to be produced.

7
SOLVING A PROGRAMMING PROBLEM

Computer programs are the instructions that are followed in processing business transactions. The programs must not only process transactions correctly, but must identify incorrect data and reject or modify it to ensure correct processing. In larger computer systems, there are thousands, perhaps even hundreds of thousands, of programmed instructions required for processing.

A computer program should be viewed by management as a subordinate. As such, it is management's responsibility to ensure that the subordinate performs the work properly. In computer systems, this is the responsibility of user management. The development of a computer system can be likened to the creation of a job description, the training, and evaluation of the program's performance. The operation and maintenance phase of the computer system is similar to the day-to-day supervision of a subordinate.

This chapter identifies the most common types of programming problems, where they occur, how to diagnose and correct those problems. Although programming is primarily a data processing function or, in many instances, is performed by a vendor and sold in a purchased application, the user must be involved in this function. If the misuse and problems associated with computer systems are to be permanently cured, that will happen only when users become heavily involved in the development of computer programs.

This chapter attempts to explain a technical aspect of data processing, in nontechnical terms. The diagnostic process has been prepared for management, and the proposed solutions are management solutions. Even the survival tactics recommended are ones that should be understandable by the nontechnician.

THE ORIGIN AND TYPES OF PROGRAMMING (SOFTWARE) PROBLEMS

Software is the term frequently applied to computer programs. Software is distinguished from the hardware, or computer, on which the software is executed. The programs are the more important of the two and represent what and how transactions will be processed.

The defects inherent in computer programs have been studied for the past twenty-five years. From these studies, we can pull together both the source of programming problems and the cause of programming problems. This background information should prove helpful to management in diagnosing computer programming problems.

Types of Program Problems

The GAO (U.S. General Accounting Office), in conducting hundreds of data processing reviews in the federal government, has identified nine major causes of software programming problems, which are:

1. *Inadequate communications between the parties affected by software design.* The development of a computer program parallels a party game. In this party game the host has a story, which the host tells the first person in confidence. This person then tells a second person, who tells a third, etc. The last person then recites the story to the group. The host then reads the original story, and everyone laughs. In a computer program design, the user tells the designer, who tells the programmer, who tells the computer. It is easy to understand how communications can break down because of many parties involved or because of the technical language associated with data processing.

2. *Incorrect perception of the nature of actual transactions to be processed.* The programmer may not understand the business and thus may not understand the purpose of a business transaction. For example, a programmer in a bank may not know thepurpose of a debit memo. In one organization that had a serious programming problem, the programmer did not know that debits had to equal credits.

3. *Inadequate documentation preventing adequate reviews of software.* The program is a highly technical piece of work. It is difficult to pick up a program and understand it easily. In some respects, it's like looking at a piece of abstract art. The more explanatory documentation, the easier it is for a supervisor or reviewer to evaluate the correctness of the computer program.

4. *Time constraints hampering the effectiveness of the design process.* Everyone seems to want processing done immediately. Just as we know nine women cannot make a baby in one month, nine people may not be able to build a system requiring nine months' effort in one month. Experience has also shown that as data processing programmers are pressured they tend to discard good control practices, such as documentation, extensive testing, and reconciliation controls.

5. *Absence of written criteria or guidelines for designers to follow.* The system design process is very similar to that of designing any other large, complex structure. For example, the analogy between the design of a home and that of a computer application is often used. Users of a computer, like families desiring a new home, like to talk about what they want. To accommodate the purchaser, the architect attempts to take those requirements and turn them into a blueprint. So does the system designer.

   When an application is being purchased, the same problem exists. Frequently, users are more interested in what the package has to offer than in what they really want. This failure to write system requirements first and then discuss the methods of implementation, bells, and whistles second leads to many dissatisfied users.

   Another culprit is the telephone change request. Too frequently, programmers take over the phone requests, which they do not fully understand, implement them incorrectly, and then take the blame for the problem.

6. *Detail and complexity involved in designing, coding, and reviewing software.* In simple, everyday terms there are a lot of things to keep track of in writing a computer system. Some people seem able to handle this large volume of detail, but others bog down in ensuring that all the pieces fit together properly. In some ways, writing a computer system is like visualizing how all the pieces in a large crossword puzzle will fit together when the puzzle is put together — without seeing a picture of the completed puzzle. Unless a detailed, methodical process is followed, it's quite easy to make design or coding errors during the developmental process.

7. *Reliance on the expertise and experience of the people doing the work (the state of the art).* Doing what the doctor or

teacher says has been drilled into many of us from early childhood. We look up to the expert in our society and accept the word of the expert as gospel. However, in any high technology, no one expert will know everything. The users of computer systems must recognize that, though they do not know a lot about technology, they do know more about the business and their own needs than the "experts" do. There is a difference between using experts and relying on them and doing everything they state.

8. *Undetected changes in circumstances make the application obsolete.* Businesses change; computer systems do not always change in the same direction, at the same time, or in the same manner. Many programming problems are associated with the fact that the computer program is processing transactions under one set of rules, while the rest of the business is using another set of rules. This can easily happen because:

   — Responsibility has not been adequately assigned
   — One party fails to inform the other party of a change
   — The user told the programmer the wrong rules of processing
   — The programmer misinterpreted what the user stated as the processing rules

9. *State of the art in software testing that prevents testing all possible conditions.* The only effective method of testing computer programs is exhaustive testing. This involves testing every possible program path. As computer systems may have millions of paths, exhaustive testing is neither practical nor economical. Therefore, all computer testing is a compromise, designed to detect the maximum number of faults at the least possible cost.

   In addition, there are very few good testing tools available on the market. Those that are available are primarily designed for large-scale IBM computers. This means that programmers individually must decide how to test, develop their test method, and then execute it. Management should also be aware that very few programmers have ever had any training in how to test computer programs. Somehow, data processing managers believe that testing is an intuitive process and therefore that all programmers must be good at it — if you believe that, I'll be happy to sell you the Brooklyn Bridge.

Sources of Programming Problems

The point at which a programming problem occurs may be far distant from the point where that problem was introduced into the program. Data processing personnel frequently refer to this as a *cascading effect*. This means that the error introduced at one point causes a problem at another point. An easy-to-understand example would be the addition of water to the gasoline tank of a car. At a later time the water will cause the engine to stop, because the cylinders won't run on water. Therefore, the problem may appear to be an engine problem, but it is really a water-in-the-gasoline problem that has *cascaded* into the automobile engine.

Studies by such organizations as IBM, Chemical Bank, and American Express have provided some interesting statistics on the cause of programming problems and the cost associated with correcting those problems. This information has been presented in Figure 25.

The graphical part of Figure 25 shows where in a computer system development process defects occur and where in the process they are detected. Note that approximately two-thirds of all the problems occur during the requirements and design phase, less than one-third occur during programming, and the rest during test and operations. About two-thirds of all the defects are detected during testing, however, and about 20 percent during operation. This means that the data processing programming staff does not detect errors at the point they occur.

Experiences in several studies, most recently by the IBM Corporation, show that it costs at least 100 times as much to correct a defect in production as to correct that same defect had it been detected during the requirements and design phase. The cost factors to fix a problem shown at the top of Figure 25 show that the cost to correct is ten times as great during testing and 100 times as great during operation.

When we combine these two factual attributes of programming, we see that there is a huge cost associated with not finding problems at the point where they are introduced into the system.

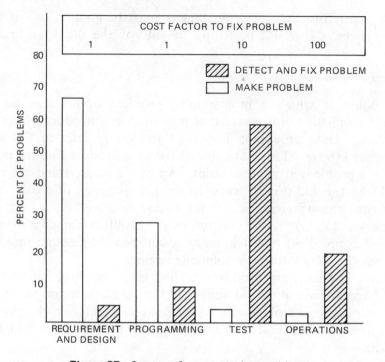

Figure 25. Source of programming problems.

Let's consider for a moment what happens when a defect is introduced during program design, but not uncovered until operation. When a defect was introduced, it was documented, designed into the system, coded, and tested. It may also have been explained in user manuals or output guides. Now problems occur with a transaction. The user must correct those problems and notify involved parties. Once the cause of the problem has been determined, the programmer must eliminate the erroneous test data, take out the erroneous program statements, change the erroneous program and system design, as well as all the documentation and user manuals. The requirements must then be rewritten; the system redesigned; the program redesigned, coded, and tested; the system redocumented; and the user issued new user manuals. It is not hard to understand why this costs 100 times as much or more than if the same defect had been corrected during the requirements or design phase of programming.

SYMPTOMS OF A COMPUTER PROGRAMMING PROBLEM

The stench of a bad computer program is no different from the smell of problems in any other part of a computer system. The programs give off the same telltale odor of foul-ups as does any other part of the computer system. In fact, many of the programming symptoms are similar to those associated with organizational problems or improper output. The cause is different, but the symptoms may be the same.

Management should not avoid facing programming problems because of their technical nature. The involvement of management is equally important and perhaps more so, because programmers may have less direct supervision than have personnel in user areas. First, programmers are considered professionals and thus are not expected to require the same level of supervision, and second, and perhaps more important to management, data processing supervisors tend to be technicians who have more interest in the technical aspect than in supervising their staffs.

The symptoms associated with programming problems are listed and explained briefly in Figure 26 and in more detail below:

- *Symptom 1 – Processing incorrect.* The outputs produced by the computer system do not contain the expected results. The cause of incorrect processing can be any or all of the following:

  - Incorrect use of programming language
  - Incorrect programming logic
  - Incorrect data
  - Operator error
  - Incorrect interpretation of correctness of processing

- *Symptom 2 – Over budget.* The cost of developing a computer program depends upon the clarity of specifications, the skill of the programmer, and the tools provided the programmer as programming aids. Excessive costs to develop a program can be attributable to any of these three factors, or they can result from a poor estimate. Occasional excessive programming costs should be considered normal, but when excessive programming costs become the rule rather than the exception, that warrants immediate management action.

NO.	SYMPTOM	EXPLANATION	SEVERITY
1.	Processing incorrect	The results produced by the computer program are inconsistent with the programming requirements and specifications	High
2.	Over budget	The cost of writing the program or installing a purchased program exceeded the estimate	Medium
3.	Behind schedule	The program was neither written nor installed at the scheduled date	Medium
4.	Purchased application requires extensive in-house modification	A purchased application was found not to meet the organization's needs after it was acquired	Medium
5.	Abnormal termination (hang-up)	The system failed to reach end of normal processing	Medium
6.	Unmaintainable code	The programmers are not able to maintain in-house-developed or purchased applications economically	Medium
7.	Startup/conversion error	The system fails to perform correctly after it has been placed into production	Medium
8.	Misuse of computer resources	A computer programmer uses more than reasonable resources in developing a computer program or installing a purchased application	Low
9.	Excessive computer time	The computer program consumes more than reasonable resources	Low

Figure 26. Symptoms of a programming problem.

- *Symptom 3 — Behind schedule.* Programming methodologies are aimed primarily at systems design and not systems management. Therefore, neither the programmer nor the supervisor has good information on the type of progress being made during development. In addition, data processing personnel tend to be optimistic by nature. The bottom line of this combination of events is that data processing project personnel may believe they can make the scheduled date until that date has almost arrived. Therefore, missing schedules should be viewed as a potentially serious management problem if it is persistent. In most cases, missing schedule is directly attributable to poor management planning and monitoring.
- *Symptom 4 — Purchased application requires extensive in-house modification.* There is some cost associated with installing any purchased computer application. It is similar to purchasing a dishwasher, in that software must be connected to the operating environment properly in order to receive the resources necessary for operation. However, if costs are not thoroughly investigated prior to acquiring purchased software, they can be exorbitant.

    The types of costs associated with purchased software that may be unnecessary include:

    - Modification to meet application in-house processing requirements
    - Change in application documentation
    - Change in application input forms/output report design
    - Modification of program code

    Most modifications to application software fall into one of three categories. The first is the interface modifications that are necessary. Second is a failure to recognize the limitations of the purchased application, which is a contracting flaw, and third is personal preference or personal desires that are generally not economical.
- *Symptom 5 — Abnormal termination (hang-up).* Computers do exactly what they are instructed to do, no more and no less. Computers also do not think or make unpredetermined corrections. An analogy that explains what can happen to a computer would be that of an individual told to take a certain route

across a bridge. If the bridge were out of use, the individual would find an alternative way across the river or ravine. A computer, on the other hand, would wait for the bridge to be reconstructed and then cross it. This process is known among computer people as an abnormal termination. Some companies, such as a major airline, began calling it a *crash*, as opposed to an abnormal termination. However, the airline management did not like the use of the term *crash* applied to anything in that business.

Abnormal terminations are easy to identify because computer processing terminates. Among the causes for an abnormal termination are:

— Improper use of the programming rules
— Improper interface between the program and the operating system
— Unending loop

- *Symptom 6 — Unmaintainable code.* An earlier discussion referred to *spaghetti code.* Unmaintainable code can also be undocumented code. The unmaintainable aspect refers to the economics of doing it, as opposed to the probability of doing it. The relearning cost in unmaintainable code is so high that the cost of changing a code becomes almost prohibitive. In addition, the probability of making errors during maintenance is significantly higher, the more difficult the program is to maintain.

The causes of unmaintainable program code include:

— Poor program design
— Use of complex computer statements, such as nested if statements
— Lack of program documentation
— Lack of programming standards

- *Symptom 7 — Startup/conversion error.* One of the most annoying and troublesome parts of computer usage to users is installation and conversion problems. These are the agonies associated with installing a new computer system. Purchasers of major appliances, such as new automobiles, are frequently aware of the problems associated with that purchase. They involve going back and forth to the service area to get annoying little defects corrected. The quality of a computer system can be judged by the number of defects encountered when new systems, purchased applications, or changes are put into production. It is also a high-risk period if large volumes of data are entered or converted from one format to another at a time a new system becomes operational.

- *Symptom 8 — Misuse of computer resources.* The computer and the aids provided to the programmer are the resources used in creating programs. The misuse of those resources results in excessive costs for program development, installation, and maintenance. Among the practices used by programmers that waste resources are:

  - Exclusive use of the computer to "debug" programs. This means that programmers never look at their work, but rather use computer resources to uncover a problem that might have been detected with a one- to two-minute review of the program instructions.
  - Testing one item at a time rather than a group of items.
  - Writing programs before they have been specified.

- *Symptom 9 — Excessive computer time.* "Computer time is cheap," everyone says, "and yet our computer bills may run into the thousands of dollars per year." A dripping faucet can add many dollars to the water bill each year. Although there is a tradeoff between people time to develop highly efficient programs and the cost of running ineffective programs, there needs to be a reasonable balance between the two.

  Programming practices that can cause excessive consumption of computer time during program execution include:

  - Execution of debugging options, such as the trace option, during production runs
  - Ineffective file structure organization
  - Calling high-usage routines from disk storage each time they are needed
  - Use of very ineffective program statements
  - Use of inefficient utility programs, such as some data base query languages, in lieu of writing efficient programs in a major language such as COBOL

PROGRAMMING PROBLEM DIAGNOSTIC CHECKLIST

Investigative pursuits are generally not as glamorous as television portrays them. The process of accumulating symptoms and factual information, summarizing and analyzing this information, and then drawing conclusions is a detailed, methodical process. Highly knowledgeable experts may deduce problems quickly, but the uninitiated must plod through a series of steps to identify the most probable cause and come up with a reasonable solution.

The diagnostic checklist for programming problems (see Figure 27) is designed to simplify this analysis process. The diagnostic checklist leads the user from the symptom identified about a programming problem to the recommended solution contained in Figure 28. Management should use this checklist in the investigation. Yes responses indicate programming problems and should be investigated to determine the actual cause, so the appopriate solution can be implemented.

CLEANUP RULE

The technician's solution to any problem is to overwhelm it with time and money. Management must always remember the mission of its business, which is probably not to have the world's best computer programs.

SOLUTIONS TO PROGRAMMING PROBLEMS

We probably know more about solving programming problems than other kinds, and yet we use those solutions less than others. Programmers like to feel creative, and the solutions appear to inhibit their creativity. What management must encourage is creativity in solving business problems, not creativity in solving technical problems.

The most effective programming solutions to computer problems are listed in Figure 28. This figure leads the user from the cause of the problem to the solution, using the problem-solving logic described in Figure 5. The specific programming solutions listed in Figure 28 are described below:

SYMPTOM NO.	ITEM	RESPONSE			SOLUTION REF. NO.	COMMENTS
		YES	NO	NA		
1	Is incorrect processing due to inadequate program testing?				1	
1	Is incorrect processing due to incorrect program logic?				2	
1	Is incorrect processing the result of failure to meet the intent of user needs, rather than the written specifications?				4	
2	Is the program over budget because of the programmers writing spaghetti code?				2	
2	Is the program over budget because the programmer is unable to debug the logic?				1	
2	Is the program over budget because the user has misused the computer resources?				3	
3	Is the program installation behind schedule because of a large number of changes?				5	
3	Is the program behind schedule because the programs are difficult to work with?				2	
3	Are the programs behind schedule because the programmer does not understand the business problems?				3	
4	Are purchased applications accepted before they have been adequately tested?				1	
4	Do the purchased applications require extensive modification because the programs are inefficient to operate?				2	
4	Is the modification to purchased applications required because the programmers don't understand how to use the resource properly?				3	
5	Are programs terminating abnormally because programmers use unusual or complex coding?				2	
5	Do programs terminate because they have not been adequately tested?				1	
5	Do programs terminate abnormally because the programmers do not understand how the computer resources, for example, operating systems, work?				3	

Figure 27. Programming problem diagnostic checklist.
(Note: Yes responses indicate potential computer problems.)

SYMPTOM NO.	ITEM	RESPONSE			SOLUTION REF. NO.	COMMENTS
		YES	NO	NA		
6	Is the code unmaintainable because it is inadequately documented?				2	
6	Is the program unmaintainable because it has made inefficient use of computer resources?				3	
6	Is the program unmaintainable because the programmer has used very complex coding?				2	
7	Are startup/conversion errors attributable to incorrect interfaces with the operating environment?				3	
7	Are startup problems due to inadequate testing of file conversions and installation procedures, such as misuse of library procedures?				1	
7	Are startup/conversion problems attributable to the fact that the quality of the programs is unacceptable to the user?				4	
8	Do the programmers misuse the programming language?				2	
8	Have the programmers misused the resources of the operating environment?				3	
8	Are the programmers misusing the computer resources by installing changes too frequently?				5	
9	Is excessive computer time expended due to an inefficient program structure?				2	
9	Is excessive computer time attributable to the use of inefficient program code?				2	
9	Is excessive computer time caused by reruns due to inadequate testing?				1	

Figure 27. Programming problem diagnostic checklist (cont.).
(Note: Yes responses indicate potential computer problems.)

NO.	CAUSE OF PROBLEM		PRINCIPLE VIOLATED	RECOMMENDED SOLUTION	
	SPECIFIC	GENERAL		GENERAL	SPECIFIC
1	Programs are not adequately tested	Complicated, costly	Simplicity	Improve	Create a test plan
2	Programs are difficult to understand and maintain and are inefficient in operation	Complicated, costly	Simplicity	Improve	Develop programming standards
3	Programmers do not understand how to use computer resources effectively	Fragmented, improper skills	Productivity flow	Change, combine	Conduct programmer training (about DP *and* the business)
4	The quality of the programs is unacceptable	Fragmented, improper skills	Productivity flow	Change, combine	Utilize a second author
5	Changes to programs are late and over budget	Poor sequence	Smooth flow	Rearrange	Adopt the release method

Figure 28. Programming problem solution matrix.

- *Solution 1 — Create a test plan.* Nothing happens well unless it is planned. Testing is the process of removing "bugs" from computer programs. A bug is a difference between a defined specification and a system result. The process of testing is frequently hit-and-miss, rather than the methodical analysis that is needed for debugging a computer program.

  A test plan should include the following:

  — Description of programs or system to be tested
  — Test conditions to be performed
  — Method of performing testing
  — Expected test results
  — Actual test results
  — Documentation of test plan and test results (this will be used during the maintenance of the program to continue testing)
  — Test opinion as to whether or not the program can be placed into production

CLEANUP RULE
An appropriate sign for a programmer's desk is "If program quality is to be, it's up to me."

- *Solution 2 — Develop programming standards.* Programming standards are a predetermined method of developing and coding programs. The standards usually indicate the method of documenting programs, the structure to follow in building programs, the programming instructions to use and not to use, as well as how to indicate and reference information within a program.

  Many of the older programmers do not like standards. They claim that they inhibit their creativity. Standards do have advantages, however:

  — Ease of turning over programs to another programmer, because both understand the rules by which the program is developed
  — Less costly maintenance

– Avoidance of difficult or troublesome situations, because they are normally excluded by the standards

Programming standards can be purchased or developed in-house. Generally, it is better to get standards from another organization and then customize them, based on the managerial philosophies of the business. It seems unrealistic for any programming organization not to use and enforce programming standards.

- *Solution 3 – Conduct programmer training (about DP and the business).* The same logic that applies to training users also applies to training programmers. Programmers need two types of training. First, they need to master the programming tools. These should be taught, and then supervisors should ascertain that the programming practices have been mastered. Second, programmers should be taught the business performed by the organization. For example, if the programmer works for a bank, the programmer should be sent to a banking school. If programmers are going to process the business's information, they need the business background to fully interpret and implement the requirements to meet the true needs of the users.

- *Solution 4 – Utilize a second author.* A second author is a quality control concept. We frequently say that an individual cannot see the trees because of the forest. Another way of putting it is when you work with the same detail for so long the obvious seems unobvious. An obvious mistake can be looked at time and again and not caught, because the primary author of the program knows it is correct and has a mental block about the correctness of that item. A second author is someone who will review the program for technical correctness as well as meeting the user's needs. Though the second author is a quality control reviewer, the second author concept implies that that individual share in the rewards and punishments associated with a good or bad program. The second author is also available to step in and take over the maintenance of the program should the primary author be promoted, transferred, or leave the organization.

- *Solution 5 – Adopt the release method.* In the early 1960s, the vendors of computer software learned the value of the release system. Before then, whenever they uncovered a problem they made a change and gave their customers a new version of a program. Sometimes this would happen weekly. The customers ended up spending more time incorporating the new versions than they saved from lost time associated with a defect. The release system predefines when new versions of a software program will become available. Unfortunately, many programming managers have not accepted this as a productivity tool.

The most common release period is three or six months. Users of computer systems must live with a particular version for that length of time. If the application is purchased, the user rarely has a choice. It is unfortunate that in-house-developed software offers that unproductive choice. Obviously, if there is a very serious flaw or an emergency demand, that will be taken care of. But the emergencies must be approved by management and the system works only when management actively discourages emergencies.

IMPEDIMENTS TO GOOD PROGRAMMING PRACTICES

An officer of a major corporation frequently referred to his programmer staff as "prima donnas." The Harvard Business School says there is a major credibility problem in U.S. industry about the data processing profession. Data processing professionals are not frequently thought of as team members, and in fact very few of them have moved up into senior management. This speaks to some of the problems inherent in the data processing profession.

The particular impediments that are frequently alluded to as stumbling blocks in developing effective business programs include:

- *Technical interests greater than business interests.* The computer should be used to solve business problems. In reality, many data processing people get their kicks from solving technical problems. They put time and effort into establishing data bases and telecommunication systems and improving computer throughput, rather than solving the true business needs of the user. One organization, in an effort to break down this technical empire, moved the programmers out into the user areas, so they would feel more closely aligned with the business than with the profession of data processing.

- *Computerese (technical jargon).* Many business people cannot speak computerese, and computer people cannot speak "business." The computer people do not understand the business, may not want to understand the business, and frequently are accused of looking down at the noncomputer people as subordinates. This attitude stifles communication and cooperation. Many users have also accused the computer people of knowing what the user's solution is without asking them. Whether the position is correct or not, it angers many users, which in turn causes communication and cooperation to deteriorate.
- *What's good for data processing should be good for the organization.* The data processing professionals frequently believe they know how to do their jobs best. Nothing wrong with this attitude, because that is why they are hired. However, their systems interface and affect other departments within the organization. It is within this interface area that most of the problems occur, and non-data-processing people can offer suggestions. In many instances, those suggestions are rejected because the data processing people know the best way to do the job. The solution they propose is for the user to learn more about data processing, rather than the data processing person to learn more about the user business.

PROGRAMMING PROBLEM SURVIVAL TACTICS

The programming system crashes, but management needs the payroll produced, invoices in the mail, or production schedule for tomorrow developed. If it takes three days to fix it, many employees may be sitting on their hands in semiretirement awaiting the computer printer to crank up and spew out the needed information.

One executive described the computer society as the IWIN society, which stands for *I Want It Now*. People are impatient and don't want to wait. Survival may mean getting it now, not tomorrow. The most common programming survival tactics include:

1. Back up to an old program version — If it worked in the past, it will work again. The difference between the processing of two versions may be less than the losses associated with not

running at all. Organizations should maintain the integrity of previous versions of a system until the integrity of the current version can be proved. It's always nice to know that if the current version fails, the company can fall back on the old version.

2. Pencil and paper processing — Some organizations have great difficulty closing their doors. For example, the U.S. Controller of the Currency gets very upset when a bank closes its door in the middle of a banking day. Therefore, when the computer goes down, the banks must keep operating. To do this, they develop backup paper-and-pencil procedures to keep them in business until the computer can be restarted.

3. Full processing redundancy — This is the Cadillac of survival tactics. Organizations that absolutely must continue processing can have that assurance only when they have two full processing systems. In some instances, those processing systems are located in different physical locations. If one system goes down, the other system can pick up immediately, like an alternative power supply.

CLEANUP RULE
If you consult enough computer experts, you will be able to substantiate any conclusion you desire. Gut feeling is frequently more valuable than the consulting opinion of a thousand experts.

8
SOLVING A TECHNICAL STAFFING PROBLEM

Acquiring a computer creates the need for staff to use it. Management has two options. First it can train the users in the use of the computer, and they can then do their own processing. Many organizations install copy machines and then let users make their own copies. This same concept can be applied to the computer. Second, management can establish a new technical function and staff it with technicians.

The staffing solution is usually based on economics. It is normally cheaper to hire a few experts for the entire organization than to attempt to create computer experts in each department in the organization. Therefore, the universal staffing solution has been the creation of the data processing department.

This new function poses a management challenge. Nontechnical management must hire and control technicians. Many senior managers have adopted a "hands-off" attitude. There is little doubt, especially based on recent Harvard Business School studies, that there are problems in many organizations between the data processing technical staff and the rest of the organization.

This chapter is designed to help senior management identify the causes of technical staffing problems. The technical players are identified, and the things that make them tick are discussed. The symptoms of problems are explained in an analytical process leading to the solution of technical staffing problems. Should serious technical staffing problems exist, some survival tactics are recommended until the longer range solutions can be put into place.

THE TECHNICAL PLAYERS AND WHAT MAKES THEM TICK

This section of the book could have been titled "Confession of an Exprogrammer." The wonderful world of EDP is different from any other part of an organization. It is a new frontier. Some of the people think of themselves as the "chosen people" of society.

Let's look first at the data processing job functions — the players. Years ago, most were trained in-house, but today there are sufficient schools to satisfy the needs of most organizations.

The more common data processing jobs are listed in Figure 29, which states job titles and a brief discussion of responsibilities. It is important to note that there are a large number of job responsibilities required to make the data processing function work. In smaller organizations, a single individual may perform two or more of these job functions, but in larger organizations the functions will be staffed as a subsection of a department. The list of job titles in Figure 29 is not meant to be exhaustive, but rather to include the more common job titles.

To most people in data processing, it is a fun profession. Earlier in the book, these people were alluded to as the high priests and priestesses of a new cult called data processing. Some articles have referred to data processing professionals as the technocrats of business. The data processing professionals often refer to their technical counterparts as "bit freaks" and "techies."

It has been correctly stated that most data processing professionals are more loyal to the data processing profession than to their companies. If asked what they do, they will say "systems analyst" and "programmer," not "work for the XYZ Company." Many are firmly entrenched in data processing and hope to spend their entire working careers within that profession.

Let's look for a moment at the three worlds in which the data processing people live, to explain where they get their kicks.

- *World 1 — Solving user problems.* The primary mission of the data processing department is to satisfy business requirements. The data processing function works on needs, such as producing payroll, maintaining accounts receivable, developing inventory control systems, etc. Generally, the business problems are identified by people called users, who then work with data processing personnel to develop automated solutions.

  This world consumes about 40 percent of the data processing resources. Perhaps that is surprising, considering that it's the primary mission, but the other worlds consume the majority of the resources. Of all job functions, the ones involved in this world are the project leader, systems analyst, and application

TITLE	JOB RESPONSIBILITY
DP Manager	Responsible for managing the data processing function
Project Leader	Responsible for developing, managing, and implementing application systems
Systems Analyst	Responsible for designing application systems
(Application) Programmer	Responsible for programming application systems
Systems Programmer	Responsible for the interface between operating software and the application system
Computer Operator	Responsible for executing the application system on the computer
Data Librarian	Responsible for storing application data
Data Base Administrator	Responsible for the organization structure and integrity of organizational data bases
Data Entry Operator	Responsible for entering application data
Quality Assurance Analyst	Responsible for ensuring the effectiveness of the process that develops and operates application systems

Figure 29. Technical players.

programmer. However, even they don't spend their full-time effort with users alone, and many times their real interests are in the technical world, as opposed to the business world.

• *World 2 — Administration and paperwork.* This is the worst of all worlds for the data processing person. It involves preparing budgets, doing work schedules, long-range planning, time reporting, project paperwork, including much of the systems documentation, and other punishments imposed on the data processing department in the form of management paperwork. Frequently, what senior management refers to as control, the data processing person refers to as unnecessary paperwork.

This world consumes about 20 percent of the data processing resources. Interesting enough, much of the paperwork is data-processing-initiated, and much of it unnecessary. Let's examine why.

Data processing professionals earn their living processing information. They love information, and they love computer systems. Therefore, they generate information about themselves and create computer systems to process that information. Just as a painter may paint his house every few years, the data processor builds systems to process information about the data processing department.

CLEANUP RULE

It has been appropriately stated that if all user work ceased, the data processing department could continue at a full workload forever. Parkinson would have loved data processing, because its own work can consume all resources. Senior management should look carefully at the internal DP workload.

• *World 3 — The technical world of EDP.* This is the most wonderful world of all. It is what makes data processing worthwhile for the data processor. This world involves acquiring, installing, and operating the computer, with all its supporting technical software systems, such as operating systems.

The types of tasks involved in the technical world include:

— Selecting system methodologies and languages
— Writing data processing standards
— Selecting, generating (that means putting together), and installing operating software
— Establishing, maintaining, and storing data files
— Operating the computer
— Analyzing and improving computer performance, and
— A host of other wonderful tasks

This world consumes about 40 percent of the data processing resources. Much of the time is necessary, because if it were not done for the department as a whole, each computer project would perform a series of individual tasks that can be more economically generated.

The question management must ponder is: If you were given a new toy (i.e., a computer) would you:

1. Rather play with that toy (the technical world)
2. Help others play with it (the business systems world)
3. Fill out reports about what you have done with your toy or what you plan to do with it tomorrow (the paperwork world)

SYMPTOMS OF THE TECHNICAL STAFFING PROBLEM

Data processing is new, highly exciting, and a profession in which the members are in great demand. With the exception of a few slow economic times, most data processing professionals can easily move to another position for the same or higher salary. However, contrary to popular belief, most data processing professionals do not move to another organization for more money. They move because:

• The computer systems with which they are currently working are a mess
• There is constant bickering among the data processing function, users, and senior management
• The organization for which they work is not using the latest data processing technology
• They are not personally growing in their field

Management, however, may perceive a problem with its technical staff because:

- Projects are over budget and behind schedule
- The data processing department does not appear to be sympathetic with the business problems
- Data processing personnel are bickering with user personnel
- Users are complaining over the integrity and quality of data processing outputs

Understanding these different perspectives, we are now ready to look at the symptoms of a potential technical staffing problem. The symptoms are listed in Figure 30, together with a brief explanation and indication of the severity of the symptom. A more detailed explanation follows:

- *Symptom 1 – Unmaintainable code.* Unmaintainable code is a symptom of the poor practice of the art of programming. It is also a sign of more junior and inexperienced people, including data processing management. It can also be considered a symptom of a staff that does not expect to remain for a long time.

  Unmaintainable code can be identified by management by any or all of the following criteria;

  – Complaints by new programmers over the status of programs they must maintain
  – User complaints over the time required to install changes
  – High frequency of problems occurring associated with system maintenance

- *Symptom 2 – High turnover in EDP.* Data processing personnel normally leave because the environment in which they work is a mess. Systems analysts and programmers encounter burnout when insurmountable problems keep growing. When asked why they leave, they invariably say "money," but some additional probing by management can usually detect the real cause.

  High turnover is a data processing management problem. It normally indicates that it is management in data processing that should be turning over, not the staff. Rarely will the problem be relieved until data processing is performed in a more orderly and structured manner.

NO.	SYMPTOM	EXPLANATION	SEVERITY
1.	Unmaintainable code	Programmers write program code that is difficult to maintain	High
2.	High turnover in EDP	More than 20 percent of the data processing staff leave in a year	High
3.	Processing incorrect	The results produced by programs are not in accordance with the program specifications	High
4.	User uninformed of change	The data processing department changes application programs and puts them into production, but does not notify the user of those facts	High
5.	No one accepts responsibility for a problem	When programs produce unacceptable results, the data processing department does not accept blame for the problem.	High
6.	EDP does not understand business needs	The data processing department personnel do not have a knowledge of the business	High
7.	Dispute between EDP personnel and user	There are continual disagreements over priorities, problems, and workload between the data processing and user staff	High
8.	Misuse of computer resources	The programming staff does not use computer resources efficiently	Medium
9.	Over budget	The products produced by data processing cost more than the estimate to produce those products	Medium
10.	Behind schedule	The data processing products are not ready on the scheduled completion date	Medium

Figure 30. Symptoms of a technical staffing problem.

Occasionally, an individual analyst or programmer will "hold up" the business for more money. The individual will threaten to quit unless salary is immediately increased. Normally, this individual is working on a critical project at a critical point in time. The solution to this dilemma is to pay the increase without question and then begin making arrangements to replace that individual as quickly as possible.

- *Symptom 3 — Processing incorrect.* Incorrect processing is defined as the difference between what should be and what is. If the program proceeds according to the specifications, the results should not be considered incorrect from a programming perspective. If the results are incorrect according to the specifications, then the programmer has performed the programming function unsatisfactorily.

  There are two general categories of incorrect processing. In the first, the results vary from specifications. This is inexcusable and should not be tolerated. Programmers of this type should be put on probation, and if their work does not improve significantly they should be terminated. The second type of incorrect processing is associated with the inability to anticipate unusual or unexpected conditions. These are the undefined specifications that the programmer attempts to anticipate. Programmers who are good at this should be rewarded, and those having problems in this area should be provided additional training.

- *Symptom 4 — User uninformed of change.* The programmer knows what goes into production and when it goes into production. If all items are included in either specifications or change request forms, the user should be informed of when those specs or requested changes are to be placed into production.

  The programmer also makes or is involved in unrequested changes. These should be limited to the operating environment, but because they present a processing integrity risk, the user should also be informed of these types of changes. Failure to inform the user of any program change is a symptom of poor working relationships.

- *Symptom 5 — No one accepts responsibility for a problem.* Data processing is a technical field. Users cannot be expected to understand what has happened when something goes wrong. The data processing personnel should accept responsibility for diagnosing the problem. If they fail to accept this responsibility, they are not performing the programming job properly. The responsibility that should be accepted is a diagnostic responsibility, which does not mean the programmer is to blame for the problem.

- *Symptom 6 – EDP does not understand business needs.* It was stated that the primary mission of data processing is to solve business needs. If the data processing staff does not understand the business, it may encounter problems in satisfying the true business needs. Without understanding, the staff will implement systems according to specifications, regardless of whether those specifications are right or wrong. It is highly likely that they will contain obvious errors that will go unrecognized due to a lack of understanding about the business of the organization.

Symptoms associated with not understanding business needs include:

- Insensitivity toward preferred customers and needs
- Failure to recognize obvious specification errors
- Incorrect prioritization of data processing work
- Failure to recognize data relationships that, if recognized, might prevent or detect obvious inconsistencies
- Failure to properly interconnect the different systems within the business

- *Symptom 7 – Dispute between EDP personnel and user.* Users depend upon the data processing outputs to perform their jobs. Generally speaking, the data processing person does not depend on the user. Data processing can build systems with minimal communication and interface between the groups. Thus, when data processing is not responsive to user needs, that can have an immediate impact on the performance of the users in accomplishing their missions.

Disputes are difficult to hide in an organization. A business, like a nation, cannot stand if it is divided. Hostile and open disputes are normally symptomatic of some deep-seated problems. If allowed to fester, they will affect the profitability of the business.

- *Symptom 8 — Misuse of computer resources.* Programmers have extensive authority over how they choose to use the data processing resources. Resources are consumed in both the creation and the execution of a computer program. The difference in efficiency between a well-designed and executable program and a poorly designed and executed one can be a factor of severalfold.

  Many data processing managers argue that one good programmer can do more work than two or three poor ones. Good programmers should be highly paid and given other appropriate rewards to ensure they stay with the business. If an individual can do two to three times the work of another individual, management should not quibble over some extra rewards for the highly productive programmer.

  Comparing the efficiency of programmers is normally easy to do, even for the inexperienced. The numbers will be significant, such as:

  - Number of programs written in a year
  - Thousands of lines of source code maintained per programmer per year
  - Average number of compiles and tests per program developed
  - Number of abends per year per programmer
  - Cost per record processed

- *Symptom 9 — Over budget.* Over budget is a management problem in data processing. The later in the development cycle that senior management becomes aware of an over budget problem, the more serious the data processing management problem.   This symptom is associated with many problem causes, but the primary cause will usually be poor data processing management. Management cannot estimate properly or cannot manage the projects so that they can be completed with allocated resources.

- *Symptom 10 — Behind schedule.* Some data processing managers guarantee that work will be done within budget and on schedule.   This is becoming a very favorable trend in data processing.   Note that many construction companies already make this guarantee about their work. It is a true professional who will stand behind a budget and guarantee a scheduled implementation date.

Making such a guarantee forces good management practices. A project will not work very many weekends or nights and permit a poor project management system to continue. If people goof, they don't mind working extra to clean up their own mess, but they do not want to put in some of their valuable personal time because the system in which they work is a mess.

TECHNICAL STAFFING PROBLEM DIAGNOSTIC CHECKLIST

One of the problems many executives face in analyzing computer problems is how to gather information. Many managers feel insecure in probing problems in a technical area. The language is one barrier to be overcome, and lack of confidence is another.

A technique that is used by investigators for this purpose is called the *shotgun technique.* This is an unstructured information-gathering technique. Prior to beginning the shotgun technique, the manager should:

1. Believe that there is a problem to be solved
2. Identify the symptoms associated with the problem
3. Have an indication of the type of information that should be gathered (note that the diagnostic checklist provides insight into the type of information that should be gathered)

The shotgun technique is for the manager who does not know where to begin the investigation. The shotgun, as its name implies, covers a wide area with small probing practices, as opposed to the rifle, which aims its full load at a specific target.

The shotgun technique begins by identifying the department or departments in which the investigation will be undertaken. The investigator begins anywhere by talking to anybody. However, it is generally more effective to talk to clerical personnel, rather than management personnel. The investigator talks to a single person no longer than fifteen minutes. The investigation is undertaken without notes and without recording responses. The type of questions include:

1. What is your job function?
2. What is the most difficult part of your job to perform?

3. Do you interface with a computer in the performance of your job?
4. What are the major helps and hindrances associated with interfacing with a computer?
5. When you have a problem with the computer system, who do you go to for help?
6. If there is a computer problem, who do you think causes it?

During the shotgun process, the investigator should talk to at least ten, but no more than twenty-five individuals. After the interviews are completed, the investigator should attempt to look for common trends and conditions as expressed by the individuals interviewed. For the uninitiated, this may appear to be a lot of idle discussion, but for the trained investigator, it is one of their most powerful investigative tools.

The questions provided on the Technical Staffing Problem Diagnostic Checklist (Figure 31) can help establish the framework for the shotgun technique. This checklist is symptom-driven and solution-oriented. Its use, coupled with the shotgun technique, provides a very powerful diagnostic process for technical staffing problems.

SOLVING TECHNICAL STAFFING PROBLEMS

The data processing manager was hired to solve technical staffing problems. If that individual is incapable of handling the problems or is himself the problem, then senior management's only choice may be to replace that individual. If that manager does some things well, but lacks some managerial skills, it may be more advisable for senior management to counsel and work with that manager rather than replace him.

Most data processing managers begin their careers as computer programmers. They have been trained in programming and other technical aspects of data processing. Their proficiency at performing technical work has led them to more and more responsibility, and eventually they have risen to manage the data processing function. To some, the Peter Principle applies, meaning that they have risen to their level of incompetence. A more realistic evaluation might be that these managers have never been trained in how to manage.

SYMPTOM NO.	ITEM	RESPONSE			SOLUTION REF. NO.	COMMENTS
		YES	NO	NA		
1	Is unmaintainable code due to the fact that the programmer has not been given prescribed programming methods?				1	
1	Has unmaintainable code been developed because the data processing function is unsure which is the best coding method?				3	
1	Is unmaintainable code developed due to lack of effective programmer supervision?				2	
2	Is high turnover in the EDP department due to user interface problems?				1	
2	Is high turnover in the EDP department due to unhappiness over the quality of data processing by users and senior management?				3	
2	Is high turnover in the data processing department due to a high frequency of changes due to the user's unhappiness with output results?				4	
3	Is incorrect processing due to lack of knowledge about the business on the part of the data processing staff?				1	
3	Are incorrect results due to ineffective testing?				4	
3	Are incorrect processing results due to the user's misunderstanding about data processing requirements and processes?				1	
4	Are users uninformed of changes because the data processing staff does not understand the impact of changes on the user's business?				1	
4	Are users uninformed of changes because there is no formal process for informing users?				2	
4	Are users uninformed of changes because the data processing staff doesn't know what type of changes affect users?				3	
5	Has management failed to define clear-cut system responsibilities?				2	
5	Are the type and frequency of problems unrecorded and summarized, making it difficult to identify problems?				3	

Figure 31. Technical staffing problem diagnostic checklist.
(NOTE: Yes responses indicate potential computer problems.)

SYMPTOM NO.	ITEM	RESPONSE			SOLUTION REF. NO.	COMMENTS
		YES	NO	NA		
5	Is it difficult to categorize a DP problem due to lack of appropriate classification criteria?				4	
6	Is the data processing staff uninformed and untrained in the business of the organization?				1	
6	Is the data processing staff unaware of the quality criteria by which systems will be evaluated?				3	
6	Has management failed to make an effort to hire or train data processing people in the organization's business?				1	
7	Are disputes between EDP personnel and user due to the lack of understanding about each other's mission?				1	
7	Are disputes between EDP personnel and users due to the failure to define quality in measurable terms?				3	
7	Are disputes between EDP personnel and users associated with differences over what data processing must produce to meet user needs?				2 4	
8	Is the data processing department unable to measure how effectively it uses DP resources?				3	
8	Is the programming and system development process inefficiently performed?				3	
8	Is the execution of computer programs inefficient?				4	
9	Are programming projects over budget due to poor development practices?				2	
9	Are projects over budget because the development procedures are ineffective?				3	
9	Are projects over budget because there are misunderstandings about project objectives between data processing and user personnel?				1	
10	Are projects behind schedule because the user keeps changing requirements?				4	
10	Are projects behind schedule because data processing does not fully understand the user mission?				1	
10	Are programs behind schedule because of poor programming practices or the inability to measure programmer performance?				3	

Figure 31. Technical staffing problem diagnostic checklist (cont.).
(NOTE: Yes responses indicate potential computer problems.)

The elements of management are planning, organizing, directing, and controlling. When these managerial functions are properly performed, the technical staffing problems seem to dissipate. Some of the solutions used in data processing in accomplishing these managerial responsibilities are listed in Figure 32. This problem-solving matrix leads from the cause of technical staffing problems through the problem-solving steps outlined in Figure 5 to a specific data processing staffing solution. These solutions are individually described below:

- *Solution 1 — Cross-train between user and EDP function personnel.* Cross-training, or cross-fertilization as it is sometimes referred to, is an awareness-type training. Once people are aware of other people's problems, they can be more sensitive and responsive to those problems. One philosopher once stated that you should never criticize an individual until you have walked in his shoes.

  The concept of cross-training between groups is easy to understand. The specific methods of accomplishing that within the data processing field include:

  — Transferring users to data processing for periods of three months to two years to train them in systems analysis and programming
  — Putting data processing personnel on internal audit teams to review user areas
  — Transferring data processing people to user areas to fortify the user department with data processing skills (note that this is usually a permanent transfer)
  — Assigning users, systems analysts, and programmers to computer operations to understand the procedures and importance of accurate and timely processing
  — Assigning data processing personnel to company task forces to address company problems other than data processing problems

- *Solution 2 — Initiate a formal system development life cycle.* The definition of quality is compliance to standards. If a completed program performs as specified, it is considered a quality program. Data processing generally suffers from a lack of good

NO.	CAUSE OF PROBLEM		PRINCIPLE VIOLATED	RECOMMENDED SOLUTION	
	SPECIFIC	GENERAL		GENERAL	SPECIFIC
1	Misunderstandings about goals, missions, objectives of other parties	Inconvenient location	Smooth flow	Rearrange	Cross-train between user and EDP function personnel
2	DP is unable to control project management	Noncompliance, ineffective	Compliance	Comply, revise	Initiate a formal system development life cycle
3	User or management dissatisfaction with quality of DP systems	Complicated, costly	Simplicity	Improve	Establish a quality assurance function
4	DP is not delivering what user expected	Fragmented, improper skill	Productivity flow	Change, combine	Establish a user acceptance test function

Figure 32. Technical staffing problem solution matrix.

standards. Part of the standards by which any system should be measured are the specific user requirements. However, another and an important part of those standards is compliance to the developmental process. We measure the quality of most items by both its functional usefulness and the structure on which it is built. For example, a house must be functionally useful, but it also must be structurally sound. The structural part requires a formal system development life cycle with good measurable developmental standards.

• *Solution 3 – Establish a quality assurance function.* A data processing department must have the tools to measure the quality of its own performance. Visualize for a moment a golfer playing on a very foggy day. The ball is teed up and hit, but the golfer does not know how far the ball goes or where it lands. Should the golfer find the ball, he is uncertain about where the hole is or how far away or maybe even in what direction. We cannot imagine the golfer not becoming frustrated quickly and quitting for the day. Now visualize computer programmers with no way of measuring how well they are doing, what the target is, or when they have gotten there. Programmers likewise become frustrated.

Quality assurance in data processing is equivalent to industrial engineering in the factory. Its objective is to improve the processes of building, maintaining, and operating computer systems. The function is performed by continually evaluating performance, identifying areas of poor performance, and then recommending improvements. Unless some individual or group has responsibility for evaluating the data processing processes, they will most likely be ignored, circumvented, or performed incorrectly. Although quality assurance need not be staffed with a full-time person, it must be a responsibility assigned to a specific individual. Quality can happen without a quality assurance function, but it rarely does.

CLEANUP RULE

Quality assurance performs a quality control function over the quality control process within data processing. Any desirable criteria, such as quality, rarely even happen unless someone is assigned that specific responsibility.

- *Solution 4 – Establish a user acceptance test function.* Testing is a quality control function. It should be performed by someone with a vested interest in the quality of the product. The users of the system are the ideal people to perform the quality control function over their data processing systems. This can be accomplished by establishing a user acceptance test function. This makes the user responsible for testing the quality of the user-requested systems and changes at selected points during development and prior to being placed into production. Note that for testing to occur, the requirements must have been defined in sufficient detail so that test conditions can be prepared.

IMPEDIMENTS TO SOLVING TECHNICAL STAFFING PROBLEMS

Earlier in this chapter, we covered the three worlds of the data processing professional. Most of the impediments to progress are associated with the difficulty in extracting the data processing staff from the technical world and getting them to devote the same time and energy to the business and administrative worlds.

The specific impediments that must be overcome in reducing technical staff problems include:

- *Satisfying the quest for technical correctness.* There is a type of survival-of-the-species instinct within data processing personnel. They feel that unless they use the most current technology their value to the business will diminish. This need to keep up to date technologically is almost an obsession with many data processing professionals. If management tends to deny them this "right," they will frequently use alternate tactics to accomplish this mission, such as attending conferences, schools, visiting other organizations, talking with the technical reps, reading and studying technical publications, etc.
- *Lack of managerial skills.* It is difficult to improve the managerial process when the manager lacks managerial skills. Many data processing managers are particularly weak at interpersonal relationships and in supervising subordinates.
- *Differences in data processing priorities.* The priorities established by data processing management may be different from the priorities established by users or senior management. Until

these priorities can be merged and a single set of priorities established, it will be difficult to make progress in areas other than those designated as high-priority items by the data processing manager.

STAFFING PROBLEM SURVIVAL TACTICS

The data processing function cannot survive long without staffing. The more orderly the developmental process, and the better the systems are documented and designed, the easier it becomes for organizations to survive without technical staff. It is almost a staffing paradox. Those organizations that are in a mess have the highest probability of the technical staff leaving and the lowest probability of surviving without that staff. Those well-run and structured data processing departments are least likely to lose staff and best equipped to survive without staff.

Should the business experience technical staffing problems, the following survival tactics have worked in the past:

1. Data processing coordinator — A coordinator, usually a member of senior management, should be assigned to oversee the day-to-day operation of data processing in the organization. This does not mean to run the data processing department, but rather to run information processing for the business. Much of the work of this individual would be to smooth relationships between users and data processing personnel, as well as to establish work priorities. If additional resources are needed, this individual should have the authority to acquire them.

2. Contract the data processing function to an outside group — This is a drastic measure in which the data processing function is dissolved. One or two people may be kept, but the entire data processing function is contracted to a third party. There are a large number of organizations that perform this service. These groups define user requirements, design and code the programs, prepare input data, and process the systems, either within the business, using contractual personnel, or in a remote location.

3. Hire a consultant to analyze and correct the problem — The problem may be beyond the expertise of senior management to identify and resolve. It may be more acceptable to parties to hire an independent consultant to analyze the problem and present proposed solutions to the business. In the case of a technical problem, the consultant should meet these three criteria:

   1. Be mutually agreeable to all involved parties
   2. Be a recognized expert in the field of concern
   3. Be able to demonstrate, through references, a record of success with this type of problem

---

CLEANUP RULE

In solving technical computer problems, one must be assured that the problem has been solved, rather than that the nature of the problem has changed.

9
SOLVING AN UNUSABLE OUTPUT PROBLEM

Have you ever ordered something from a store, been handed a bag, and then discovered after you got home, that either the wrong product was in the bag or not every item ordered was in the bag? Did you ever take your automobile in to be repaired and drive it home with the same problem still present? Did you ever order something through the mail and have it arrive broken? If you can answer any of these questions affirmatively, you will know how users of a computer system feel when their output reports are wrong, missing, or incomplete.

This chapter addresses the detection, prevention, and correction of computer output problems. These output problems are the dissatisfiers of the data processing field. Though they cannot be completely eliminated, they must be reduced to an acceptable level.

The chapter identifies the symptoms by which senior management can detect computer output problems and then proposes solutions for those problems. The chapter leads management through the diagnostic process to the cause of the problem and then the solution. The impediments to solving output problems are defined as are the survival tactics needed to produce usable results until the problems can be fixed.

THE DATA PROCESSING EXPECTATION GAP

The power of the computer is not the processing ability of the machine, but rather the ability of individuals to break complex tasks down into small pieces. Visualize for a moment attempting to teach a two-year-old child how to tie shoelaces. The process takes an adult only a few seconds, but may be a time-consuming, frustrating task for a two- or three-year-old. Visualize further having to write out instructions on how to tie shoelaces. Now you can appreciate some of the challenge of computer programming.

The computer, though a marvel of engineering, can do only three basic tasks:

- Move data (into, within, and out of the computer)
- Compute mathematically
- Compare two values (determine whether one value is higher than, equal to, or lower than another value)

These three instructions, when properly assembled, can produce a program to guide a rocket to the moon, produce a weekly payroll, or determine economic quantities for purchasing, but at the same time it can underbill 500 customers within one minute. Putting together hundreds or even thousands of instructions in the proper sequence is a challenge for even the best programmers. Even the best can rarely deliver a defect-free system.

The source of a lot of data processing problems is people's perceptions or expectations of what the computer system will do. There is a belief fostered by many data processing people that the computer can do anything. Users are led to believe this, and then when the realities of life occur the system results fall short of inflated expectations.

This gap between what the data processing department actually delivers versus what the user expects is commonly referred to as the *expectation gap* (see Figure 33). When a project or change commences, there is a tentative meeting of the minds as to what the system will do.

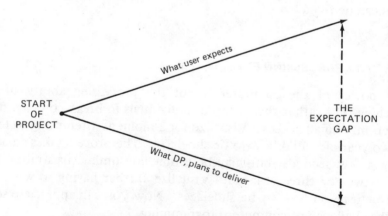

Figure 33. The data processing expectation gap.

As development begins, the users and the data processing staff firm up in their minds what the end product will be. Frequently, the user's expectation drifts in one direction, toward perfection, while the data processing project must create the system within available resources and may therefore make compromises that the user may or may not know about or understand.

If the data processing function cannot close this expectation gap, there is great dissatisfaction with system outputs. The cause of the problem may be real or perceived. For example, the results may be actually erroneous or they may just be presented in a different format or reliability from those expected by the user.

Without some definition of quality, the user will expect perfection, and the data processing department will be unable to deliver. With expectations too high, the user is certain to be disappointed. Once disappointment sets in, the self-fulfilling prophecy begins. This means that the user expects bad results, looks for bad results, and finds them. This is not an excuse for poorly designed systems, but rather for urging that realistic expectations be defined and then measured. For example, it may be realistic to expect that invoices will be priced correctly 99 percent of the time. If they are, then the quality of output should be considered acceptable. If not, changes should be made.

SYMPTOMS OF AN UNUSABLE OUTPUT PROBLEM

Unusable output is that output for which the user says, "I can't use that $%*!/X$ output!" In other words, unusable output is information that is unacceptable to the user. However, this should be considered a managerial problem only when it is outside the normal expectations of the system. Above, we talked about invoices being produced correctly 99 percent of the time. If fewer than 1 percent were incorrect, the system would be performing in accordance with the correctness tolerances, and therefore any problem should be dealt with using normal system procedures. It is those variances that exceed system tolerances that warrant managerial attention.

The symptoms management should look for as indicative of unusable output outside the predefined system tolerances include:

- *Symptom 1 — Out-of-balance reports.* The totals produced by the computer report are either incorrect or inconsistent with

NO.	SYMPTOM	EXPLANATION	SEVERITY
1.	Out-of-balance reports	The information contained on the report does not balance to a control total	High
2.	Errors in computer output	The information contained on an output report is wrong	High
3.	Input data lost	Data received by the organization is not included in computer processing	High
4.	Input data wrong	The data recorded by the computer system is in error	High
5.	Processing incorrect	The results of computer processing do not comply with the specifications for processing	High
6.	Output data lost	Information processed by the computer is not delivered to the user	High
7.	Manual adjustments made to computer output	The user makes some manual change to the computer output before it is used	Medium
8.	Duplicate records maintained by user	The user maintains some or all of the information that is readily available from the computer system	Medium
9.	User complaint	The user expresses dissatisfaction with the usability of computer output	Medium
10.	Startup/conversion error	The system is either incorrect when it is placed into production or the process of placing it into production generates errors	Medium
11.	Changes required on short notice	The user requests an immediate change dealing with the unusability of output	Low

Figure 34. Symptoms of an unusable output problem.

externally maintained control totals. From a user perspective, the integrity of the report is in doubt. It is generally unwise to use any computer-produced output until the integrity of that information can be proved.

The types of out-of-balance conditions that the user might find include:

— Input entered is not in balance with batch totals
— Columns of figures do not total to the computer-produced totals
— Computer-produced totals do not match to manually maintained totals
— One computer system total does not agree with another system total of the same information

• *Symptom 2 — Errors in computer output.* The information printed about the processing of individual business transactions is in error. This presupposes that erroneous input has been caught by the system rules and rejected. That is not to be considered erroneous output. Errors in processing acceptable data represent computer output-type errors.

Among the more common output errors are:

— Wrong names (e.g., products, customers, etc.)
— Wrong prices for products
— Wrong codes or percentage rates
— Inconsistencies between two related variables (e.g., a pay rate outside the range of an employee's pay grade)
— Misplaced decimal point
— Failure to indicate negative values
— Misspelling
— Acceptance of erroneous input

• *Symptom 3 — Input data lost.* Data lost prior to the initial control point is outside the prerogative of control. For example, if an order is lost in the mail there is little a business can do about it. However, when the input reaches the control point, its presence should be validatad throughout the processing cycle. If that data is lost, it should be of great concern to the business.

The reasons that data can be lost after the first control point include:

— Careless handling by employees
— Batches lost in transmission, such as in the company's internal mail
— Data lost at a hardware/software failure
— Data lost due to system deficiencies

• *Symptom 4 — Input data wrong.* The major challenge to correct processing is the correctness of input data. Some of the largest and most complex programs in computer systems are those validating the correctness of input data. These validation programs can eliminate only input data that violates the system processing rules. It is possible to pass the processing rules and still be incorrect. For example, a customer may want one gross of 144 products, but indicate that he wants 144. The computer system will ship 144 gross, which is wrong, but because the quantity is numeric it passes the system validation rules.
    Examples of wrong input data include:

— Data outside normal system rules, such as alphabetic characters in a numeric field
— Erroneous data that meets processing rules, such as the previous example of a gross of products
— Invalid or unauthorized transactions, such as a transaction being entered twice or into the wrong system

• *Symptom 5 — Processing incorrect.* The processing rules within the program are incorrect. In these situations the input is correct, but the error occurs within the computer system. The common types of errors include:

— Incorrect master data used for processing, such as a wrong product price
— Rounding error in processing
— Incorrect program logic (this type of error produces large numbers of errors in a single computer run)
— Wrong version of program or data used for processing

• *Symptom 6 — Output data lost.* Input entered into the computer is processed correctly, and output is prepared. The output never reaches the intended user of that information. Reasons that output data can be lost include:

— Delivery to wrong department or individual
— Careless handling on the part of computer operations
— Hardware/software failure, resulting in failure to transmit or print
— Intentionally or unintentionally destroying or removing reports

- *Symptom 7 — Manual adjustments made to computer output.* Errors in output reports can be addressed by any of the following three options:

  1. Leave as is (can be done if error is small or inconspicuous)
  2. Return to data processing for correction and reprocessing
  3. Make manual adjustments to the computer output

  The alternative selected will be dependent upon the time and effort required to make manual adjustments.

- *Symptom 8 — Duplicate records maintained by user.* Cowards do not trust data processing systems. Many banks that update customer accounts during the day via on-line terminals reprocess those same records at night in a batch mode. Until users can build their confidence in computer systems, many maintain duplicate records. However, this is indicative of potentially serious system problems and a potential huge waste of resources for the business.

- *Symptom 9 — User complaint.* As things get worse, users of data processing systems complain more. The first complaints tend to be directly to the data processing group. If action is taken, the complaints tend to die away. If the system does not improve, the frequency and loudness of complaints increase. Also, complaints begin to be made to senior management, as opposed to operating management. When this happens, it is almost certain that a significant mess exists.

- *Symptom 10 — Startup/conversion error.* Any time a new system is placed into production there is a high probability of problems. The newly introduced processing has not been tested under fire. Just as many people dread getting a new automobile because they hate to debug it, users frequently dread changes or new computer systems. The quality of computer systems can be judged by the number of defects uncovered when new systems or changes are introduced into production.

- *Symptom 11 — Changes required on short notice.* The data processing department usually complains about short-notice requests. This symptom can mean either that there is a serious problem in the computer system or that the user has not adequately planned changes. Regardless, it is a symptom of a potential problem requiring investigation.

UNUSABLE OUTPUT DIAGNOSTIC CHECKLIST

Computer problems can turn senior management into full-time investigators. All chief executive officers need a few major computer problems to test their character. If senior executives have successfully avoided the computer until the first major crisis, they will find themselves thrown into the fire quickly. Some problems must be solved instantaneously, while others can be reviewed at a more leisurely pace.

One investigative technique that can be used is called the *bump-on-the-log* technique. This technique is called *surveillance* by investigators. The objective is to go to some inconspicuous location and then observe the types of activities that are occurring in the area being investigated. Professional investigators can use such techniques as wire tapping, which are not available to the private sector.

Executives can use the bump-on-the-log, or surveillance, technique in any of the following manners as they investigate the activities of data processing:

- Semipermanent residence — The executive temporarily moves into the data processing department and observes activities. This can be done under the pretext of studying manuals, looking at reports, etc. With this technique, the investigator asks no questions, just sits until the individual's presence no longer causes concern and then notes the activities that are occurring.
- Unannounced visits — The executive can make a habit of coming into data processing periodically. This may even be several times a day. This is a sampling version of the previous method. The investigator notes what is going on at each visit.

- Wastebasket/desk drawer method — After working hours, the manager goes through the wastebaskets of data processing and through the desks of the data processing staff. The objective is to determine what is being done by the evidence produced by the various activities in the data processing department.

  This technique has advantages and disadvantages. Obviously, it is a type of spying and, if known, may cause resentment on the part of the data processing staff. Nevertheless, the technique gives management some additional insight into the potential causes of data processing problems.

In the investigation of unusable output, the types of items to be investigated are included in the Unusable Output Problem Diagnostic Checklist (Figure 35). This, like the other checklists in this book, is not meant to be exhaustive, but rather representative of the types of items that indicate computer problems. The checklist items should be supplemented based on the user's personal experience and the problem being investigated. This diagnostic checklist is meant to be the path leading from the symptoms listed in Figure 34 to the solutions indicated in Figure 36.

UNUSABLE OUTPUT PROBLEM SOLUTIONS

It is highly probable that the first report produced by the first computer system contained errors. The economics of perfection is mind boggling. The real question is how far an organization is willing to back down in quality.

The concept of an acceptable level of error is a difficult one for many managers to comprehend. We hate to tolerate mistakes and yet are not willing to afford the cost of zero defects. We do know that unrealistic expectations may cause as many problems as a reasonable number of errors can cause.

The solutions used by the better data processing organizations to minimize the unacceptability of output include:

- *Solution 1 — Create a control clerk position.* A control clerk is an individual in the data processing department responsible for the accuracy, completeness, timeliness, and reasonableness of computer input and output. This can be a full- or part-time function.

SYMPTOM NO.	ITEM	RESPONSE			SOLUTION REF. NO.	COMMENTS
		YES	NO	NA		
1	Is the out-of-balance condition because the detail in the computer report does not equal the computer-produced total?				4	
1	Is the out-of-balance condition a difference between the computer-produced and the manually maintained control total?				1	
1	Is the information from an input batch lost?				1	
2	Is the error on the report obvious to the casual observer?				1	
2	Has this error occurred before?				2	
2	Was the output error due to an input error?				1	
3	Was input lost in the user area?				4	
3	Was input lost in the data processing area prior to processing?				1	
3	Was input lost during processing?				1	
4	Is the input error obvious to the casual observer?				1	
4	Is the input error an unanticipated error?				3	
4	Is the input error a repetition of the same error made in the past?				2	
5	Is the incorrect processing obvious to the casual observer?				1	
5	Does the processing error cause the control totals to be out of balance?				4	
5	Is the processing error unanticipated?				3	
6	Was output lost in the data processing area?				1	
6	Was output lost en route to the user area?				1	
6	Is the reason for the lost output a repetition of a previous cause of loss?				2	
7	Are manual adjustments made because the problem occurring was not anticipated?				3	
7	Were the problems requiring manual adjustment not identified prior to giving the report to the user?				1	
7	Are manual adjustments made after the fact because the integrity of the output could not be proved at the time of delivery?				4	

Figure 35. Unusable output problem diagnostic checklist.
(NOTE: Yes responses indicate potential computer problems.)

SYMPTOM NO.	ITEM	RESPONSE			SOLUTION REF. NO.	COMMENTS
		YES	NO	NA		
8	Are duplicate records maintained because the user cannot prove the integrity of the computer output from that output?				4	
8	Are duplicate records maintained because the user is unsure what might go wrong?				3	
8	Does the user maintain duplicate records because the user does not believe others share in that responsibility?				1	
9	Do users complain about the inability to prove the integrity of computer-produced data?				4	
9	Do users complain about obvious errors not being caught in the data processing area?				1	
9	Do users complain about the same type of errors repeating run after run?				2	
10	Are startup and conversion problems due to data file problems?				4	
10	Are startup and conversion problems not identified by the data processing department?				1	
10	Are the same types of startup and conversion problems occurring regularly?				2	
11	Are changes required on short notice because the integrity of information cannot be verified at the time output is produced?				4	
11	Are changes required on short notice because the problems addressed by the change have not been anticipated?				3	
11	Are the changes by the user required on short notice because the data processing department did not anticipate a problem?				1	

Figure 35. Unusable output problem diagnostic checklist (cont.).
(NOTE: Yes responses indicate potential computer problems.)

	CAUSE OF PROBLEM		PRINCIPLE VIOLATED	RECOMMENDED SOLUTION	
NO.	SPECIFIC	GENERAL		GENERAL	SPECIFIC
1	Inaccurate or incomplete data is being sent to users	Noncompliance, ineffective	Compliance	Comply, revise	Create a control clerk position
2	The same type of error recurs periodically	Noncompliance, ineffective	Compliance	Comply, revise	Use an error-reporting form (and summarize results)
3	Problems are not being anticipated	Noncompliance, ineffective	Compliance	Comply, revise	Utilize risk analysis exercises
4	The integrity of the DP systems is difficult or cannot be proved	Noncompliance, ineffective	Compliance	Comply, revise	Require the establishment of simple accounting proofs in each application

Figure 36. Unusable output problem solution matrix.

One of the important lessons of control is that if nobody is responsible for an area, nobody cares whether the area is performed correctly or not. Accountability has always been one of the major building blocks of control. Only single individuals can be accountable, groups cannot.

The control clerk should be someone other than the computer operator or the programmer. For each application processed on the computer, a single individual would have responsibility for:

— Ensuring that all the expected input has been received (e.g., if batch numbers are used, the individual accounts for all batches)
— Preparing all tapes, disks, and output printer forms for the computer run
— The application being run on a timely basis
— Verifying any processing control totals produced
— Scanning all reports for reasonableness
— Scanning all reports based on scanning criteria provided by either the application programmer or the user
— Ensuring that the output and input are afforded the proper security
— Ensuring that the outputs are delivered to the user on a timely basis
— Ensuring that any transactions rejected by the system are delivered to the appropriate individual for correction and reentered on a timely basis

• *Solution 2 — Use an error-reporting form (and summarize results).* One of the quality principles is to investigate every defect, no matter how small. Though all defects may not be corrected, they should be investigated. Also, where defects are repetitive, their combined impact is much greater than any single defect.

Defects can be dealt with only when they are documented. Most organizations find that a standard form for documenting problems achieves the following pruposes:

— Substantiates facts because they are recorded
— Facilitates communication because there is a basis for discussion

- Ensures that the defect will be investigated because it is recorded and controlled
- Ensures that there will be a response that facilitates cooperation because the user's problems are being attended to

- *Solution 3 — Utilize risk analysis exercise.* A risk analysis exercise is an exercise in negative thinking. The objective is to attempt to identify what might go wrong and the potential magnitude of that threat. The objective is to ensure that the most probable threats are or will be dealt with by the system.

  The risk analysis exercise is not a time-consuming process. It is a type of brainstorming, but is directed toward the what-can-go-wrong aspect of systems. The traditional data processing approach is to identify what is needed (i.e., a positive approach) and then to accomplish those objectives. In using this approach, the potential threats are frequently overlooked.

  The most logical participants to a risk analysis exercise are:

  - Data processing project leader
  - Experienced data processing professional, perhaps the DP manager
  - One or more user clerical personnel involved in the area
  - One or more user supervisory personnel involved in the area
  - Individual with risk experience, such as an auditor, CPA, consultant, or security officer

  The risk analysis exercise is a three-part exercise, as follows:

  - Part 1 — Explain system or area being investigated, which defines the scope of the exercise. This part should also explain how risk analysis is performed.
  - Part 2 — Identify as many possible risks that might result in losses to the area being analyzed.
  - Part 3 — Determine the potential loss associated with each threat. Note that some organizations describe loss only in terms of high, medium, or low.

  At the end of the exercise, this list of risks, together with the magnitude of each risk, can be given to the data processing project team. It will determine whether system controls adequately address the risk and, if not, review with the user the need to add controls for the risks of concern.

- *Solution 4 — Require the establishment of simple accounting proofs in each application.* A simple accounting proof is as follows:
  - Start with beginning balance from the last computer run
  - Add the value of new transactions this computer run
  - Subtract transactions that have been completed or otherwise satisfied
  - Produce ending balance at the end of each computer run

  For example, in accounts receivable, we would start with the old accounts receivable balance, add charges to customers' accounts to that balance, subtract payments and other credits, arriving at an ending balance. The ending balance can then be used to verify the integrity of the processing information before any output reports are produced. This simple procedure can solve a huge number of data processing problems. It is surprising how few data processing applications use the simple accounting proof. Perhaps it is not so surprising, because very few accountants are involved in the development of computer systems.

CLEANUP RULE

What you can't measure in a data processing system, you cannot control. It is important to determine how the integrity will be measured, so that the appropriate controls can be established.

IMPEDIMENTS TO ELIMINATING UNUSABLE OUTPUT

It would appear incomprehensible that there could be impediments preventing the usability of computer output. Unfortunately, there are. The most obvious impediments are:

- *Cost to improve quality of outputs.* Everybody wants to drive a Cadillac, but not everybody wants to afford it. How often do we drive our automobile into a service station only to be told that a tire needs replacement or we need some other costly repair job. All of a sudden we are willing to live with risks that we said we didn't want to live with. Note that this area must be studied carefully to ensure that all costs and benefits are included. Bad quality decisions can be made if the information is not accurate and complete.

- *Insufficient priority to fix.* Many of the unusable output problems are minor. When these are stacked up against the other changes awaiting implementation, some of the problem output conditions may be given a low priority. This impediment is not one of not doing it, but rather of deciding when it should be done.
- *Don't know how to fix it!* The cause of unusable output may be known, but the method of correcting it may be beyond the comprehension of the people involved in the system. If we look at our earlier example of a user indicating the wrong quantity on the order form, we know that this produces unusable output, but we may not know how to get the user to provide the correct output. Many of these types of mistakes must be lived with.

UNUSABLE OUTPUT SURVIVAL TACTICS

In many instances in data processing, the cure is worse than the illness. For example, in our last impediment, the cure might be not to deal with certain customers. This can solve a computer problem, but it might create a huge business problem. Determining the solution in many areas is more a matter of economics than a desire to correct.

If unusable output is produced, the user might consider some of the following survival tactics as a way of surviving until tomorrow, when things may get better:

1. Attach notice of error to report — If the error is universal or minor or obvious, the purpose of the report may be achieved by notifying the user of the report of the problem. For example, if an invoice had the wrong due date on it, you could attach a notice saying "we goofed" and then indicate the appropriate due date. This will make some unusable output reports usable with minor inconvenience to the user.
2. Redo manually — This survival tactic has been suggested for several other problem areas. All it is saying is that in some cases people are more flexible than machines. It's also nice

to be able to say that occasionally people can replace machines, and perhaps the machines can go to the unemployment lines for a while.

CLEANUP RULE
A plan of action to correct a situation always occurs at the point where management tires of studying the problem.

10
SOLVING A DISASTER SITUATION

The continued growth in dependence on computers and on the data processed by them has increased the importance of plans to prevent loss of their availability. In some organizations it is still reasonable to consider recourse to manual operations when automated data processing systems become unavailable. Today, there are fewer and fewer situations in which it is even possible to revert to manual operations. When it can be done, the cost in lost time and confusion might be, and usually is, unacceptably high. Thus, contingency plans are necessary to minimize the damage caused by unexpected and undesirable occurrences.

The probability of the occurrence of an undesirable event is generally inversely related to its magnitude. Usually, the greater the catastrophe, the lower the probability that it will happen. In other words, data processing operations are disrupted with far higher frequency by small problems than by large ones.

There is another relationship that, though not obvious, is quite important to the quality of contingency plans. The size, or scope, of a catastrophe and its effect on data processing operations are often not directly related. In the absence of a good plan, minor damage can cause major problems. Conversely, with a good plan, even major damage may not result in serious losses.

This chapter describes an orderly process for generating and using a contingency plan. The information contained in this chapter is not intended to be an all-inclusive source of information on contingency planning. The objective is to describe contingency planning, explain the symptoms of inadequate contingency planning, and then, through analysis, determine the solution to those plans. Some survival tactics are offered for organizations that currently do not have a contingency plan.

DISASTER RECOVERY STRATEGIES

The development of a contingency plan to minimize the damage resulting from losses or damages to the resources or capability of an

EDP facility depends for its success on recognizing the potential consequences of undesirable happenings against which the facility needs protection. The facility is an assemblage of many resources. Some particular subset of these is needed to support each function provided by the facility. These resources include, but are not necessarily limited to, people, programs, data, data processing hardware, communications facilities, power, environmental control, the physical facility and access to it, and even paper forms.

All resources are not equally important, nor are they equally susceptible to harm. Thus safeguards, including the elements of a contingency plan, should be selected with informed awareness of which system functions are supported by each resource element (devices, programs, data, etc.), of the susceptibility of each element to harm (accidental or intentional), and of the consequences of such harm. In short, cost-effective protection of a data processing facility depends heavily upon:

- An awareness of its relative dependence on each of its component parts;
- Knowing at least in an overall way what the chances are that something undesired will happen to each component;
- A determination of the ramifications of such things happening, so that, finally;
- Things can be done to minimize either the chances of them happening, the loss if they happen, or both.

The maximum permissible cost of any safeguard is limited by the size of the expected losses that will be mitigated by that safeguard. Any safeguard or combination of safeguards must not cost more than tolerating the problems to which the safeguards are addressed. Satisfying these goals clearly requires identifying the losses expected as a consequence of undesired things happening to resources. Such a process is called *risk analysis.*

In addition to providing a basis for the selection and cost justification of security measures, risk analysis provides data on time as a factor in assessing the possible consequences of losses of security. Knowing the consequences of not being able to perform each system function for specific time intervals is essential to creating contingency plans that are adequately responsive to the needs of the supported organizations.

With very few exceptions, a large percentage of an EDP facility's workload is deferrable for significantly long periods of time without unacceptable hardship. There is usually only a small percentage of the workload that must be run, because its delay would cause intolerable disruption. It has proved very difficult to guess reliably and accurately into which category each data processing activity should fall. It is also very difficult to guess very accurately the maximum tolerable delay for the processing of each deferred activity. A properly conducted risk analysis yields this data, which can then be used to justify or reject contingency plan elements based on actual, quantitatively expressed needs of the supported organizations for EDP services.

A contingency plan is based on several categories of assumptions. Most can be established only after a quantitative risk analysis. The whole list of assumptions for inclusion in the document cannot be completed until well along in the planning cycle. Included in the set of assumptions should be the following:

- *Nature of the problem.*

  - The general nature and range of events against which the plan is directed.
  - Events not addressed by the plan that, because of their low probability, do not warrant consideration in the plan.
  - Events that are so extensive in scope as to negate the need for early recovery of data processing operations.
  - Events too minor in scope to warrant reflection in the plan. These are generally sufficiently frequent as to be considered a normal part of the operation and are not accommodated routinely.

- *Priorities.* Senior management and midlevel EDP management have a critical need to understand how priorities are determined. The data sources, the extent of user management on the selected priorities, the risk analysis methodology, and other related matters should be described in detail adequate to a full understanding of the relative priorities to be observed in recovery of operations and of the rationale used to establish those priorities. In many organizations the relative criticality of the supported functions will vary with time of day, day of week, and day of month. Where appropriate, the description of priorities should reflect that situation.

- *Commitments to or assumptions of support.* Recovery from any but minor, and relatively frequent, problems usually requires assistance in some form from groups beyond the immediate control of the EDP management. The assumption of such support, including notes of formal commitment by other organizations, difficulties in getting commitments, and related matters should be addressed. The list of the assumptions relative to resources might include the following:

  − Availability of replacement hardware and licensed software.
  − Availability of supplies possibly influenced by transportation problems in the event of a major problem.
  − Utilization of another EDP facility and its formal commitment of support.
  − Availability of people of all categories. (We frequently overestimate the mobility of employees after a natural disaster, particularly when that mobility requires leaving their dependents in less than desirable circumstances.)
  − Response of public utilities, particularly if there is a natural disaster of some kind.
  − Availability of funds, including indication of gross amounts and possible sources.

With relatively few exceptions, the selection of appropriate strategies should follow the risk assessment. Until the risks are assessed, it is usually difficult to know the critical functions that must be maintained and the demands for resources that will be made to support those critical functions. Thus, it is expected that the strategy can be, at least tentatively, selected immediately after the risk assessment is complete. EDP and organizational management, as appropriate, should determine the basic strategy to be followed. Suggested strategic alternatives follow:

- *Strategy 1 − No hardware backup.* A few organizations need an EDP facility to perform their mission, but will not be seriously harmed if they are completely without it for periods of time possibly as long as two weeks. It is the nature of these operations that they are rarely, if ever, dynamic, transaction-

oriented, communications-dependent shops. In these few cases
in which dependence on EDP is not immediate and critical, it
is not unreasonable to assume that the original hardware can be
repaired or replaced at the current or another location in time
to avoid major loss, provided only that other dependencies,
such as people, data, and programs, are suitably protected
through backup procedures. Belief that backup of hardware
facilities is not required does not provide justification for
ignoring contingency planning. Further, a sound risk analysis
must support the conclusion that no backup arrangement is
required.

• *Strategy 2 — Mutual aid agreements.* Mutual aid agreements
are at least conceptually possible when one facility can accept,
without serious harm to its supported organizations, the critical
work of another temporarily inoperative facility. Technically
practicable transportability of work between two facilities
requires the data and programs from one be acceptable to the
other without other than the most modest change, and prefer-
ably no change at all. Rehearsals are essential, but they are
usually costly and generate unwelcome disruption to the shop
providing backup. The rehearsals must include full operability
of the critical functions of the facility that is down. These
practice sessions or rehearsals must be thoroughly realistic
and not, for example, depend on the use of any resources from
the inoperative facility for operation at the backup site. These
are very difficult to conduct in a mutual aid environment. To
assure compatibility with the backup system, it is highly recommended that critical functions be run (daily, if necessary) at
the backup facility as part of the normal job stream (with test
data, files, etc.).

It is difficult at best to make mutual aid arrangements
totally reliable. Changes in either system (a highly likely
occurrence) may instantly render the arrangement invalid.
Further, management shifts may invalidate the arrangements
without prior notice, leaving a previously supported facility
without backup.

Although mutual aid agreements are conceptually feasible,
they rarely, if ever, prove workable where needed. The penalty
to the supporting shop of discovering in time of need that

backup is not actually available is generally too great to warrant confidence in this strategy.

- *Strategy 3 — Contingency centers.* Contingency centers are facilities established to provide a location into which an EDP organization that has lost its own facility can move temporarily to reestablish its complete or critical functions. These centers may be cooperatively owned by several organizations to back up the owners' facilities, or they may be established as profit-making ventures that sell rights to their use through membership fees, dues, and other charges. The evolution of these centers is still quite recent — too recent, in fact, for there to be a large body of experience to support their workability or to provide guidance on the potential pitfalls to be avoided. Determining the feasibility of using such centers is not complex, does not seem to have hidden pitfalls, and thus should be relatively easy to do if based upon the results of the risk assessment. There are many situations in which such centers may well be the most cost-effective route to go, while there are others in which they are not an appropriate means of backup. Again, the decision must be made on a facility-by-facility basis.
- *Strategy 4 — One facility, more than one location.* This is achieved by having EDP in two geographically separated locations, the smaller of which is large enough to carry the critical workload for the few days needed to reestablish the inoperative facility. This strategy does not imply the installation of excess capacity great enough to carry the critical work — only the physical dispersion of the normal capability into two or more locations. The economic feasibility of this is based on the frequently confirmed assumption that, for the majority of facilities, the critical workload is less than 50 percent (commonly less than 20 percent) of the total load, so that no increase in total EDP capacity is required. Hardware often does not divide cleanly into two halves, but there is usually no requirement to have precisely 50 percent at each site. Any split that will suit the need for processing the critical work at either location is adequate, provided, of course, that the backup facility converts its workload to include only its critical functions.

Realizing all the potential benefits of the two-location option requires that both locations have full capability to run the critical workload. This generally requires availability of the full range of essential skills to be available at each site. This might, but does not necessarily, mean significant added costs. However, the feasibility of this depends heavily on the size of the operation being considered. Some shops are sufficiently large that it is now difficult to argue that any economy of scale they might provide outweighs the increased costs of the bureaucratic processes in an operation that size.

SYMPTOMS OF A DISASTER RECOVERY TIME BOMB

Disasters are situations that disrupt computer processing. The disruption can be minor, such as loss of electrical power, or major, as a result of flood, fire, or earthquake. Implicit in a disaster is the lack of forewarning of what will happen or the severity of the problem.

The only thing certain about computer disasters is that they will happen. The third thing a data processing manager can count on in life, in addition to death and taxes, is a disaster. In most instances, it is the procedures undertaken by the data processing department that determine whether or not the disaster will have a serious impact on the business. Senior management may not be aware of the continual string of disasters happening within the data processing department. In some organizations, disasters are an everyday occurrence. The more common types of disasters occurring in a data processing department are:

- Improper computer operator action
- Abnormal termination of processing
- Power failure (a surge or loss of power for a fraction of a second can cause serious problems)
- Hardware malfunction
- Operating software malfunction

The signs that disasters are occurring and may not be adequately planned and addressed include (see Figure 37 for a summary of disaster situation symptoms):

- *Symptom 1 – Input data lost.* Disasters can occur in many ways that cause data transmitted to the computer center to be lost, including communication line failures, computer system

NO.	SYMPTOM	EXPLANATION	SEVERITY
1.	Input data lost	Data supplied by users is lost during a disaster	High
2.	Processing incorrect	Problems occurring during a disaster result in incorrect processing results	High
3.	Files lost	One or more versions of a computer file are destroyed	High
4.	Lack of backup data	When computer data is lost due to a disaster, there are no backup versions of that data	High
5.	System abuse for personal gain	The cause of the disaster is sabotage by personnel	Medium
6.	System abuse – unintentional	The disaster is caused by some improper act performed unintentionally	Medium
7.	Misuse of computer resources	Excessive resources are used either to prevent or to recover from a disaster	Medium
8.	Excessive time to recover	Users are denied processing results for excessive periods of time	Medium
9.	Overtime work in DP department	The computer operations and programming personnel must work extra hours to recover from a disaster	Low

Figure 37. Symptoms of a disaster situation problem.

failures, hardware and operating software failures, carelessness, theft, and natural disaster. Two items are important from a user perspective in regard to the loss of input data, which are:

1. The loss is detected on a timely basis
2. Adequate backup data is available to replace the lost data

Note that in many instances the data processing department will not know that input data has been lost, because it will not know about data that was lost before it was logged in to the data processing control records.

- *Symptom 2 — Processing incorrect.* Incorrect processing occurs when either the disaster or the extent of the disaster is not known. For example, a surge in electrical power may change the values of data stored within computer memory. If the surge in power is not detected by a hardware control, the bad data may be processed, producing incorrect results. Good control practices should catch these types of problems. However, catching them after the fact indicates inadequate disaster detection controls.

- *Symptom 3 — Files lost.* One of the more serious disaster problems for organizations is the loss of a computer file. Some of the reasons that a computer file can be lost include:

  - File written on a disk device, but the hardware is unable to read the information back
  - Data is improperly written over the top of data, destroying all or parts of the computer file
  - Hardware device destroys computer file, such as might happen with a bad write head or read head on an input/output device
  - Operator incorrectly uses a computer file as a work file for another system
  - Programming, software, or hardware problems cause the integrity of a file to be lost during processing

Lost files pose many problems to an organization. The larger the file, the more time that will be consumed in re-creating it. The longer after the disaster that the problem is uncovered, the longer it will take to recover the file. There is also a concern that adequate backup will be available for reconstructing the file.

- *Symptom 4 — Lack of backup data.* Backup data is information retained solely for the purpose of reconstructing processing. The information can be used for audit trail purposes, to explain how transaction processing occurred, or used to reconstruct lost or damaged computer files. There is a cost associated with saving backup data. These are primarily the costs of the data media, the storage area, plus the administrative effort to maintain a library of backup data.

    The challenge with backup of disk files adds a fourth dimension, namely, the resources required to transfer the information on the disk file to a backup file. With large files, this can take many minutes or even hours of computer time to create a backup. The dilemma is the tradeoff between computer time to make backup copies of the disk files, versus the time required to recover, which grows in length as fewer and fewer copies are made of the disk files. The solution to this dilemma is normally the decision on how quickly the data processing center must recover after a computer file disaster.

- *Symptom 5 — System abuse for personal gain.* One of the major causes of computer disaster is sabotage. This means that an individual deliberately destroys the integrity of computer processing, not for financial gain, but more for revenge or the challenge of doing it. If employees feel unfairly reprimanded, dislike their supervisors' attitude, or fail to get what the employees feel to be fair raises, the employees may take frustration out on the organization through sabotage of computer resources. Sabotage can be performed by:

    — Deliberately damaging the hardware, such as bending a read or write head on an input/output device
    — Taking or destroying computer media
    — Entering erroneous data designed to hang-up the system
    — Altering the sequence or instructions given the computer to cause it to malfunction

    The difficulty with sabotage is that it is normally indistinguishable from poor computer practices or normal equipment malfunction. IBM states this is an area of growing concern among its customers. Average employees become more computer-knowledgeable and thus are better equipped to take out personal frustrations on the business's computer. Sometimes sabotage is done for the mere enjoyment of beating the system.

One large insurance company, when it sent its notice of dividends to its policyholders, offered three options for the policyholder. From the viewpoint of the insurance company, the least desirable was to return the dividend in the form of cash to the policyholder. As a practical joke, when the option selection notice was printed, a computer operator added this sentence to the policyholder notice: "If you select option 3 [the option to return cash,] the company will break your fingers." This type of playful sabotage, though humorous to the operator, was not humorous to company management, which received a large number of irate phone calls from the policyholders.

- *Symptom 6 — System abuse — unintentional.* More damage will be done to the computer through incompetence than any other reason. The less training and supervision provided in the computer center, the greater the probability of unintentional problems. Any of the types of disasters that can be caused intentionally can also be caused unintentionally.

- *Symptom 7 — Misuse of computer resources.* Disasters can consume large amounts of resources. It is not uncommon after a minor disaster has occurred to incur a major disaster during the corrective process. One large dairy products company, after a minor disaster involving the loss of a computer file, lost all the backup accounts receivable files during the recovery process. This misuse of computer resources cost the company hundreds of thousands of dollars in uncollectible receivables, as it was unable to reconstruct the accounts receivable file. It is essential that procedures ensure that the recovery process does not cause more problems than were encountered in the original disaster.

- *Symptom 8 — Excessive time to recover.* The time between the occurrence of the disaster and the time when the integrity of processing is recovered is lost time to the user. Some users are able to continue for extensive periods of time without computer assistance, though others are out of business the moment the computer goes down. In some businesses, the longer it takes to recover the computer system, the more business that might be lost. The time span for recovery should be a system requirement, and procedures should be developed to achieve those recovery time requirements.

- *Symptom 9 – Overtime work in DP department.* Disaster recovery consumes resources two ways. First, computer personnel must work to recover the integrity of the system that has been lost due to a disaster. Second, once integrity has been restored, then the processing that has not been performed during the disaster period must be performed. If a disaster lasts for a very long time, the amount of overtime required to recoup can be extensive. Overtime hours worked is usually a good measure of the number of disasters and the efficiency with which the computer center can recover from a disaster.

DISASTER SITUATION DIAGNOSTIC CHECKLIST

Analyzing the adequacy of disaster recovery planning and procedures requires a knowledge of the objective of such a plan. At a minimum, contingency planning is needed to:

- Assure that all important areas of information processing are addressed
- Create procedures that are easy to follow
- Provide for training and evaluation of computer center and user staffs in disaster recovery
- Permit ease of reference to sections of immediate interest or concern
- Facilitate revision by minimizing the effect on the whole document of changes in limited areas of concern

Another area that must be probed is the knowledge of all affected individuals about the plans and their roles in the contingency plan. An essential element of an effective contingency plan is unwavering insistence that all persons on whom there is significant dependence during contingency operations be familiar with their potential prospective roles. The challenge of contingencies is that rarely will two disasters be identical. Each one poses a unique challenge, which is no time to begin to determine how to recoup operations.

The disaster procedures must not be based on the assumption that the document describing the recovery procedures can be retrieved after the disaster by each person with a role in the recovery. Those individuals will then read the plan and learn how to do what is needed of them. It should not be necessary to read the plan to initiate contingency operations.

To assist management in analyzing past and potential disasters, a Disaster Situation Problem Diagnostic Checklist (Figure 38) follows. This diagnostic checklist builds off the symptoms of management concern about disaster situations. Yes responses to the items included on the checklist are symptomatic of conditions that need correction. The solution reference number column refers to the recommended solutions for disaster problems, which are listed in Figure 39 and described later in this chapter.

CLEANUP RULE

Whenever a disaster occurs, it will occur at exactly the wrong moment. Contingency plans should handle the worst-case situation.

DISASTER SITUATION PROBLEM SOLUTIONS

EDP facilities generally provide a service to one or more functional areas of their organizations. Occasionally, they provide data processing support to several organizations. Recognizing that the EDP shop is a support operation, not an end in itself, is essential to the proper conduct of many aspects of data processing management. It is no less important to the generation of realistic, cost-efficient contingency plans.

Because the EDP facility provides services of which some are usually vital to the organization, the senior management of each organization should realize the critical nature of that organization's dependence on contingency plans that serve to keep within tolerable limits the consequences of losses or damage to EDP resources. Economic feasibility in contingency plans requires carefully derived decisions as to what organizational functions are deferrable and for how long. As described later, the costs of these deferrals should be established.

SYMPTOM NO.	ITEM	RESPONSE			SOLUTION REF. NO.	COMMENTS
		YES	NO	NA		
1	Is input being lost before control is established in the data center?				2	
1	Is input data being lost during computer processing?				4	
1	Is data being lost due to inadequate performance of recovery procedures?				5	
2	Are processing controls inadequate to detect incorrect processing resulting from disasters?				3	
2	Is incorrect processing due to the inability to reconstruct input data?				1	
2	Is incorrect processing due to the lack of recognition of disaster risks?				3	
3	Are files lost due to inadequate disaster recovery procedures?				4	
3	Are files lost due to the improper performance of disaster recovery procedures?				5	
3	Are files lost because the disaster recovery plan did not address the types of problems that are occurring?				3	
3	Are files lost because there is inadequate backup for reconstruction?				2	
4	Has the user failed to provide adequate backup of input?				2	
4	Has the data processing area failed to provide adequate backup of its data?				2	
4	Is there adequate backup of data in an off-site facility?				1	
5	Are unauthorized people allowed in the computer area?				3	
5	Is the cause of any DP disasters unknown?				3	
5	Can people access computer resources in the event of a disaster without having accountability for that act recorded?				4	
6	Are individuals who might be involved in disaster untrained in how to perform their functions?				5	

Figure 38. Disaster situation problem diagnostic checklist.
(NOTE: Yes responses indicate potential computer problems.)

SYMPTOM NO.	ITEM	RESPONSE			SOLUTION REF. NO.	COMMENTS
		YES	NO	NA		
6	Is the disaster recovery plan left unmaintained, so that the procedures are not current?				3	
6	Are controls inadequate to detect or prevent the more common types of computer disasters?				4	
7	Are records indicating what individual used what computer resources unavailable to pinpoint accountability in the event of a problem?				4	
7	Is the workability of the disaster plan untested?				5	
7	Has the organization failed to develop disaster procedures outlining the steps to be performed and who performs them in the event of a disaster?				4	
8	Has the user of any system failed to indicate the time in which recovery must be performed?				4	
8	Have the priorities for recovering systems in the event of an extensive disaster not been established?				4	
8	Does data processing have inadequate resources to recover in the specified recovery time span?				4	
9	Is overtime in the DP department attributable to the lack of a disaster plan?				4	
9	Is overtime in a DP department associated with disasters due to the lack of training and testing?				5	
9	Is overtime in a DP department associated with a disaster due to the inadequate backup of computer data?				2	

Figure 38.   Disaster situation problem diagnostic checklist (cont.)
(NOTE: Yes responses indicate potential computer problems.)

NO.	CAUSE OF PROBLEM		PRINCIPLE VIOLATED	RECOMMENDED SOLUTION	
	SPECIFIC	GENERAL		GENERAL	SPECIFIC
1	All the DP eggs are in one basket	Inconvenient location	Smooth flow	Rearrange	Establish an off-site data library
2	Data is unavailable for use in recovery	Poor sequence	Smooth flow	Rearrange	Create backup copies of data
3	No one is assigned disaster recovery responsibility	Fragmented, improper skills	Productivity, smooth flow	Change, combine	Establish a disaster recovery committee
4	The recovery process is a disaster	Complicated, costly	Simplicity	Improve	Establish a disaster recovery plan
5	The disaster recovery procedures do not work properly	Complicated, costly	Simplicity	Improve	Test and maintain the plan

Figure 39. Disaster situation problem solution matrix.

It is practically impossible for such decisions to be reached entirely within the EDP organization. The EDP management is not usually in a position to assess accurately the relative importance to the whole organization of work done by the respective supported areas. Further, the relative cost of continued support of each in the face of adversity may vary quite widely. Thus, cost of support under unusual conditions must be considered. For these reasons, it is not only appropriate but very important that the senior management provide direction and support for contingency planning to the end that the organization continue to provide essential functions following disruption of the EDP facility. Senior management should do the following:

- Direct the establishment of contingency plans that are based on the results of a comprehensive risk analysis.
- Direct support of the planning process by all functional areas servicing and serviced by the EDP facility. In particular, identify those functions that are critically dependent upon the EDP facility. Of extreme importance is the assistance of supported activities in identifying those vital records and data maintained by the EDP function, i.e., those that are essential to the sustained continuation of supported activities following a disruption of service or destruction of the EDP facility.
- Direct initial and periodic later tests of the workability and costs associated with the plan.
- Direct periodic revision of the plan as a consequence of information derived from the tests and as a result of changing dependence of the organization on EDP. Likewise, the plans should be completely reviewed upon reaccomplishment of a risk analysis or a change in any of the critical dependencies.

The process of review and approval for a contingency plan should be carefully established to satisfy several important objectives, as follows:

- Make top management aware of any dependencies upon it for supportive action.
- Obtain management agreement on the assumptions on which the plan is based, including the dependence on other organizations for assistance.

- Communicate to management the existence of a plan, and obtain approval of the plan.
- Obtain formal concurrence of certain other organizations upon which there might be dependence.
- Through required reading and acknowledgment by signature (usually on a separate card), inform key employees of their respective roles in the various recovery scenarios.

The specific solutions relating to disaster recovery are listed in Figure 39. This problem solution matrix traces the problem situations identified on the diagnostic checklist (Figure 38) to the cause of those problems, to a specific solution using the problem-solving logic described in Figure 5. Note that these solutions need to be customized based on the degree of risk associated with the loss of computer resources to the business.

- *Solution 1 – Establish an off-site data library.* To recoup from a computer disaster, any or all of the following resources will be needed:

  1. Computer hardware and communication facilities
  2. Application programs, operating software, and operating procedures
  3. Computer data

  Of the three resources, computer hardware and communication facilities are the easiest to replace. The programs, procedures, and data may not be replaceable if the computer site is destroyed by a disaster, unless those resources are stored off-site.
  It is good practice for all data processing installations, regardless of size, to store data and programs off-site. These off-site facilities can be:

  - Other locations of the same business
  - Residences of key company officers
  - Special storage facilities designed specifically for off-site computer data storage
  - Banks or other custody agents

The frequency of transferring data to and from the off-site storage will vary based upon the importance of that information. As a general rule, it should be done weekly.

- *Solution 2 — Create backup copies of data.* The information to be stored in an off-site facility, as well as an on-site storage facility, is the backup data. Although many data processing functions adequately protect their computer files, they forget to back up some of the following:

  — Input source documents in the user area
  — Updated versions of computer programs
  — Computer operator procedures
  — Operating system software and the interface parameters connecting application programs to the operating system

- *Solution 3 — Establish a disaster recovery committee.* A golden rule of data processing, which bears repeating from previous chapters, is that things do not happen unless a single individual is held responsible for performing a specific task. Disaster recovery is no different. One individual, normally the computer center manager, should be held accountable for disaster recovery procedures. However, data processing personnel cannot by themselves adequately plan for disaster recovery. This is because much of the work and the areas to be included in the plan are known only by operating management. The solution to this is to form a permanent disaster recovery committee comprising the individuals having a vested interest in disaster recovery. The committee should be chaired by the manager of computer operations.

- *Solution 4 — Establish a disaster recovery plan.* A disaster recovery, or contingency, plan is the key ingredient to recouping from a disaster. Earlier sections of this chapter explained the strategies, approaches, and areas to cover in a disaster recovery plan. The following questions designed to be answered yes for a good disaster recovery plan, provide for a minimal self-assessment of the adequacy of the disaster recovery plan:

  1. Does the plan include both manual and automated segments of information processing?
  2. Has the plan been customized to the organization?

3. Is the plan well documented and understood by the participants?
4. Has the plan been reviewed and approved by senior management?
5. Is the plan up to date?
6. Has the plan been tested?
7. Are the procedures straightforward?
8. Do the participants have confidence in the adequacy of the plan?
9. Does senior management have confidence in the adequacy of the plan?

- *Solution 5 — Test and maintain the plan.*   One of the more important aspects of successful contingency planning is the continual testing and evaluation of the plan itself.   Quite simply, a plan that has not been tested cannot be assumed to work; likewise, a plan prepared, tested once, and then filed away to wait the day of need provides no more than a full sense of security.   Data processing operations are, historically, volatile in nature, resulting in frequent changes to equipment, programs, documentation, customer requirements, and often even in the way daily business is conducted.   These actions make it critical to consider the plan in the same context (i.e., a frequently changing document).   A plan quite adequate today may be woefully unsatisfactory two months, or less, from now.   Suffice it to say, if the EDP contingency plan is not subjected to continual and rigorous management review, as well as in-depth testing on a scheduled basis, it will fail when needed.

IMPEDIMENTS TO AN EFFECTIVE DISASTER RECOVERY PROGRAM

Disaster recovery is not an exciting topic to everybody.   There is a tendency to believe that disasters that have not occurred in the past will not occur in the future.   For this reason, fewer than 15 percent of all people in automobiles use seat belts.   The reasoning is that they have not been in an accident in the past and therefore will probably not be in an accident in the future.

It is interesting to note that people who have had disasters become fanatical about those disasters in the future.   Those who have been in serious automobile accidents use seat belts regularly. Those organizations that have had serious fires conduct regular fire drills. Organizations that have not experienced a specific disaster rarely put much time and effort into preparing for that disaster.

The impediments to disaster recovery are basically lack of interest in spending money for something that may not happen. The specific impediments that must be overcome include:

- *The it-hasn't-happened-here-before syndrome.* One disaster recovery expert said there was a twenty-year disaster law. The law stated that if a disaster of the type being considered had not occurred in the last twenty years, the feeling was that it would never happen. Because most data processing organizations are less than twenty years old, if the type of disaster being uncovered has not occurred, the concerned parties may have difficulty getting management interest in expending money for disaster recovery.
- *Inability to agree upon the magnitude of the risk.* Experience has shown that it is difficult for management to quantify the magnitude of a potential disaster. For example, if computer operations were to be shut down for a twenty-four-hour period, exactly what might that cost the business? Equally difficult to estimate is the frequency of disasters. Were both the value and frequency known, the annual impact of a disaster could be quantified, which would make decisions easy. However, without knowing the magnitude of a disaster, it is easy to underestimate it and make the wrong decision regarding preparing for that potential disaster.

COMPUTER DISASTER SURVIVAL TACTICS

Without planning, a business may not survive a computer disaster. Although to date the cause of a business failure has not been directly attributable to a computer disaster, the probability looms greater in the future, as businesses place more reliance upon computer processing. No survival tactic can take the place of a well-developed and tested disaster plan, but the following tactics may help ease the burden of a disaster, until a plan can be developed and tested.

1. Awareness of the concern — Many people new to the computer area are unaware of the potential damage that can be done to a business through a computer disaster. If the participants, including users, are made aware of the risk, they may be able to take measures or mentally prepare for a disaster situation. Tactics as simple as making an extra photocopy of a source document, batching and storing source documents in the user area, or being more aware of problems can help lessen the severity of a disaster.

2. Carry home key files and programs — The key to survival in a lot of disasters is having the survival information. These are copies of current programs, recent data files, and operating procedures. As the data processing department goes to a new version of a file, a manager may take that previous version home and store it until the next version is ready. This not only provides backup data, but protects the organization from threats or sabotage by key data processing personnel.

3. Buy insurance against disasters — Computer disaster insurance is available, but costly. This should tell us something about the need to prepare for disasters, if insurance companies are reluctant to insure against it. If a business feels it is very vulnerable to a disaster and has yet to establish a well-developed and tested disaster plan, it should consider paying the price to protect itself until it has adequately developed, customized disaster procedures.

CLEANUP RULE

The following laws seem to hold true about disasters:

1. If the disaster plan addresses six items, the seventh will cause the problem.
2. Nothing is as easy to fix as it appears to be.
3. No solution is as effective as a well-thought-through and tested plan.

11
SOLVING A SPACE MANAGEMENT PROBLEM

The United States Occupational Safety and Health Act addresses the number of square feet of space that need to be allocated for a worker. The more workers that are crowded into a work area, the less effective the work process becomes. Crowding causes more interaction, more interruptions, and perhaps more waiting to use certain resources. The same analogy holds true for storing data within the space allocated.

Space management does not sound like a subject that should cause problems, and particularly it is not a subject that should interest senior management. However, space management in many organizations is the major cause of problems and is one of the leading causes of inefficient performance of data processing systems. The problem is basically technical in nature, but some of the solutions are administrative.

This chapter attempts to explain the space management problem in data processing. Because it is a problem many managers will hear, they should have a general understanding of it. The chapter also identifies the symptoms of a space management problem, which may appear long before a manager is alerted to the cause of a problem. As some of these symptoms represent several problems, an analytical process is provided to determine whether or not it is a space management problem and, if so, how to solve it. Because computers cannot run when they are out of space, some survival tactics are suggested to help alleviate an immediate problem until a longer term solution can be developed.

WHY A SPACE MANAGEMENT PROBLEM?
— AND IF THERE IS A PROBLEM, WHAT IS IT?

In the early days of computers, files were contained on punched cards and computer tapes. These files were basically unlimited in length, but had the disadvantage that to get to any record in the file you had to begin at the beginning and read all the records up to the one that was wanted. If a large number of records were wanted, and the accesses could be done sequentially, this file structure posed no problem.

As computer technology advanced, the demand grew for accessing single transactions or records at a time. This was made possible through the introduction of disk storage, which works like a long-playing record. Just as the needle on the record can be transferred to select any specific track easily, so can the read head on the disk be transferred to locate any specific transaction easily. The problem with disk is that its size is finite; card files can be extended by adding more cards, and tape files extended by adding more reels of tape. This practice does not work with disk files, even when the disk space is removable, because the time and effort to change disk packs or diskettes would make the practice impractical.

Many computers today use only disk files, which poses the following two system design problems:

- Problem 1 — Finite limit to disk space: Because the space is limited, only a certain amount of information can be placed on that storage area. When it is exceeded, either data will be lost or processing will have to stop.
- Problem 2 — Need to locate specific records: A method has to be established to find the desired record. This is normally an index, such as the list of songs on each side of a long-playing record. The more data contained in a disk file, the larger the index becomes.

Disk files can be used in one of two manners. First, they can be dedicated to the use of a single user. For example, a disk file can be used exclusively for payroll purposes. Second, a single disk file can be used by multiple users. For example, a file in a bank can contain all the information about a single customer and thus would be used by the tellers, mortgage department, loan department, and credit card department.

As the use of disk storage becomes more sophisticated, the problems of designing and managing the use of that space become more complex. For the simple dedicated disk files, the application programmer can establish the structure and maintain the file. As more users begin to use the same file, the complexity increases geometrically.

The solution in the data processing area has been to establish a new speciality. This is the data base administrator job, which was described in the technical staffing chapter (Chapter 8). The data base administrator is responsible for organizing and maintaining data for use by application programmers. Note that in smaller organizations the data base administrator may not be a full-time job, but it is a specifically assigned responsibility.

The difference between a dedicated file and a data base is the difference between the retrieval system one has in one's desk and the retrieval system established in a large public library. The data base administrator is the librarian for computer data stored on a disk file.

The bottom line of all this to management is potential problems it never even dreamed of. Visualize for a moment sitting at a computer terminal when the message "out of space" appears. Visualize your marketing manager calling you and stating that the company can't accept any more customers because they are out of disk space. Visualize your billing manager telling you that you can't invoice your customers this week because billing can't occur until space has been reorganized. Avoiding these types of situations occurs through a function called *space management*.

The concern about space is mismanagement, not management. With proper management, problems don't occur. With mismanagement, all sorts of problems occur.

SYMPTOMS OF A SPACE MANAGEMENT PROBLEM

When you are out of space, you are out of space. That's rarely a symptom, it's a fact. However, crowds build up slowly, and the symptoms of the problem occur long before the last inch of space disappears.

Space problems are such an everyday occurrence in data processing that they frequently are not viewed as serious problems. If you live in a city with polluted air, you begin to think all air is like that until you get out into the country. This just means that sometimes the problem exists, but the data processing staff cannot see its true magnitude.

The symptoms that senior management can look for that indicate space management problems include (see Figure 40 for a summary of the symptoms):

- *Symptom 1 — Abnormal termination (hang-up).* One of the major causes of abnormal termination is the inadequacy of space. If a particular work area or file is designed to hold ten records, processing will stop when the eleventh record is processed, because there is no storage space available. Computer systems are designed to recognize these out-of-space problems, and stop processing so that space can be reallocated.
- *Symptom 2 — Terminal lock-up.* Operators of computer terminals will periodically experience data management problems. Some of these problems will be directly attributable to lack of sufficient space for data. For example, in the movement of large amounts of temporary data to permanent storage, the operator may find inadequate space available to store the information. The lack of adequate space can also degrade processing to the point where it may appear that the terminal is nonresponsive to an operator request.
- *Symptom 3 — Inadequate computer time.* It is not uncommon in some disk files for over one-half the disk space to be used for indexes. It seems almost incomprehensible to a noncomputer person to visualize a hundred million positions for storage, of which fifty million are allocated for indexes. It might sound as if Parkinson designed the access mechanism, as the overhead seems to expand to consume the available space. Others state that as the vendors make computers cheaper and faster, they must find schemes, such as elaborate indexing methods, to consume that extra capacity.

As the indexing schemes become more complex, and space begins to fill, the level of service degrades. In some systems, this degradation is slow, though in others, when a certain space threshold is achieved, service degrades quickly. It's possible for a system to be giving a four-second response at one moment and a short time later to take two minutes to respond.

It is even possible with some sophisticated file organization structures that at certain points the overhead consumes all the available processing time. The data processing people call

NO.	SYMPTOM	EXPLANATION	SEVERITY
1.	Abnormal termination (hang-up)	The computer stops due to the lack of space to put data	High
2.	Terminal lock-up	The individual on-line to the computer is unable to continue processing because of a space problem (Note: Sometimes the computer message does not indicate the proper cause)	High
3.	Inadequate computer time	The available computer time is consumed due to inefficiently structured disk files	High
4.	Input data lost	When space problems do not cause abnormal termination, the data involved may be lost	High
5.	Processing incorrect	If data is lost due to inadequate space, the totality of processing will be incorrect	High
6.	Manual adjustments made to computer outputs	Adjustments need to be made, because data is either lost or incorrectly processed due to space management problems	Medium
7.	Request for additional hardware	When more disk space is needed, one solution is to acquire more disk hardware	Medium
8.	Overtime work in DP department	The shortage of available space requires reallocation and reorganization of disk space, which may require overtime	Low

Figure 40. Symptoms of a space management problem.

this *thrashing*. What it means is that when someone changes a single record the system overhead may have to change literally thousands of indexes pointing to that particular record.

- *Symptom 4 – Input data lost.* You can't put more data into an area than there is space available. Computers themselves develop survival tactics to handle such a situation. One of the tactics is to stop, which has been discussed earlier. Another tactic is to keep placing the last record in the space allocated for the last record. For example, if room has been allocated for ten records, the first ten records are placed in the file. The eleventh is put into the spot where the tenth was, the twelfth is put into that same spot, and so on. If fifty records were processed, the first nine would exist, and the fiftieth record would be in the spot where the tenth record was supposed to be. Records eleven through forty-nine would have been lost. Normally, messages are prepared indicating the situation, but these can be easily overlooked if the computer does not terminate processing.

- *Symptom 5 – Processing incorrect.* Space management problems can lead to the loss of data, truncation of data, or incorrect arrangement or structure of data. All these problems can lead to incorrect processing. The processing results are incorrect because the data being processed is incorrect. Thus, a *Catch-22* situation.

- *Symptom 6 – Manual adjustments made to computer output.* If space problems are known, adjustments can be made for identified problems. In our previous example, we talked of space being allocated for ten records. Let us assume there were eleven, so that one record was lost, but it was known. The processing involved for that record, such as preparing an invoice, could be performed manually.

- *Symptom 7 – Request for additional hardware.* Requests for additional disk storage devices are an obvious clue to a space management problem. In some instances, the problem can be solved with additional hardware; in other instances, more hardware is dealing only with the symptom, not the problem. One of management's real dilemmas in the computer field is to ensure that when it approves requests it is solving problems, not treating symptoms.

- *Symptom 8 — Overtime work in DP department.* The reorganization process for disk storage can be a very time-consuming process. One state agency has gotten into a bind in which it takes more than two full days to reorganize disk storage. Because the agency cannot shut down for more than two days at a time, it cannot possibly reorganize at any time. The only solution is to buy more and more hardware and still watch performance degrade.

Good space management techniques require someone knowledgeable in both data processing and the business. If only the data processing aspects of space management are addressed, the cause of the problem may still exist. The use of overtime, though frequently necessary to alleviate space management problems, should be watched closely if it persists.

SPACE MANAGEMENT DIAGNOSTIC CHECKLIST

One of the lessons auditors have learned about auditing the data processing area is not to bluff their way through the review. There is a tendency not to want to feel inferior to those being questioned. One way auditors used to bluff was to incorporate data processing jargon into their questions and speech. Mustering all the fortitude they could, it took approximately twenty-seven seconds to detect an auditor who was bluffing from one who knew what he was doing. Retaliation in kind being a natural response, many data processing professionals led auditors down the wrong path into making unrealistic recommendations that could easily be shot down by the data processing staff.

This investigative message is brought to you by an ex-data-processor who used to lead auditors down the wrong path. Those auditors who had a job to do and who worked in a cooperative manner got exactly what they needed. Senior management must adopt the same attitude. If managers are required to manage and control data processing, they will need to probe and inquire about data processing problems.

Management should perform its probing from a position of strength, rather than technical weakness. It is suggested that they acknowledge the technical weakness, but also deal with their strengths, which are:

- An authoritative position, being senior in the organization to the data processing staff being reviewed
- A better understanding of the business and the business problems
- A better understanding of the type of risks and the potential impact of the risks facing the business
- Being in a position to act once the cause of the problem is recognized
- Knowing that most data processing problems are not technical but people problems

Building on this position of strength, a diagnostic checklist for analyzing symptoms of a space management problem is presented in Figure 41. This checklist represents the items that, if not present (receive a yes response), indicate problems whose solutions are referred to in Figure 41 and stated in Figure 42.

SPACE MANAGEMENT PROBLEMS SOLUTIONS

A very popular consultant is one who can solve space problems without building factories, warehouses, or office buildings. We frequently use space very ineffectively, because when there its use appears to cost nothing. If space is sitting idle and we utilize it, it does not appear to cost our business any more than if we didn't utilize it. Unfortunately, there is a moment of truth with space. When more is needed, it is very costly to acquire. It's at those points and times that we begin to rethink the effective utilization of space.

If you were to hire a computer space consultant to come in and advise you how to use space more effectively, the consultant might recommend any or all of the following solutions:

- *Solution 1 — Assign space management responsibility to computer operations.* Application systems, such as payroll, use disk space to run the payroll system. Therefore, doesn't it appear obvious that the people in charge of that system should also be in charge of space. If we followed that same philosophy we would let the company storing goods in a public warehouse store those goods anywhere it wants. This would not pose a problem until we ran out of space, at which time we would have

SYMPTOM NO.	ITEM	RESPONSE			SOLUTION REF. NO.	COMMENTS
		YES	NO	NA		
1	Did system processing terminate because the application programmer was unaware of the forthcoming lack of space?				1	
1	Are there frequent space management problems causing abnormal terminations?				2	
1	Is the organizational structure of the file such that it causes frequent abnormal terminations?				4	
2	Has insufficient file space been allocated to avoid terminal operator lock-up problems?				4	
2	Do terminal lock-up problems involve application programmers in order to solve the problem?				1	
2	Is the frequency of terminal lock-up due to space management high?				2	
3	Is the efficiency of disk file processing inadequate?				3	
3	Do computer operations personnel have difficulty restarting a system after a space management problem?				1	
3	Do some space management problems require more hardware to solve?				4	
4	Do messages fail to indicate when no more space is available for processing?				3	
4	Does the system fail to indicate when processing is beginning to degrade?				3	
4	Is processing other than the terminal program causing space problems stopped after a space problem has occurred?				3	
5	Is the frequency of space management problems unknown?				2	
5	Are computer operations personnel unable to fix space problems that have caused incorrect processing?				1	
5	Are space problems that affect the accuracy of processing unanticipated and unexpected?				4	

Figure 41. Space management problem diagnostic checklist.
(NOTE: Yes responses indicate potential computer problems.)

SYMPTOM NO.	ITEM	RESPONSE			SOLUTION REF. NO.	COMMENTS
		YES	NO	NA		
6	If manual adjustments are made, are they made without information produced by the computer system about space allocations?				3	
6	Is it normally necessary to make manual adjustments due to space management problems?				2	
6	Is it difficult to rerun quickly systems experiencing output problems due to space management limitations?				1	
7	Are restructuring alternatives for disk files ignored before new hardware is requested?				4	
7	Are the causes of inefficient processing of disk files unknown?				3	
7	Does the DP area fail to calculate the expected increase in processing perform-ance before new hardware is requested?				2	
8	Are reorganization times for files unplanned?				3	
8	Does the DP area fail to monitor the fre-quency of abends due to space manage-ment monitored, and when that fre-quency is higher than desirable to take appropriate action?				2	
8	Are computer operations personnel un-able to correct space management prob-lems as part of their normal job respon-sibilities?				1	

Figure 41. Space management problem diagnostic checklist (cont.).
(NOTE: Yes responses indicate potential computer problems.)

	CAUSE OF PROBLEM		PRINCIPLE VIOLATED	RECOMMENDED SOLUTION	
NO.	SPECIFIC	GENERAL		GENERAL	SPECIFIC
1	Programmers must be called in at all hours to fix space problems	Fragmented, improper skills	Productivity flow	Change, combine	Assign space management responsibility to computer operations
2	Abends due to space problems are high	Noncompliance, ineffective	Compliance	Comply, revise	Monitor space usage and file access performance
3	Some disk files are very inefficient	Noncompliance, ineffective	Compliance	Comply, revise	Develop reorganization policies and procedures
4	The solution to space problems is always to buy more hardware	Noncompliance, ineffective	Compliance	Comply, revise	Utilize space management models and simulators

Figure 42. Space management problem solution matrix.

to call in the people and ask them to rearrange their merchandise so we can get more product in the public warehouse.

The solution in the public warehouse, just like the solution with computer disk space, is to hire a manager to manage the space — all the space, not just the space for a single customer or computer application. The individual most qualified to do this would be a person resident in the public warehouse, or resident near where the computer disk space is physically located. In the computer field, this is someone in computer operations. Most organizations that have experienced extensive computer space management problems come to this solution.

- *Solution 2 — Monitor space usage and file access performance.* As stated before, what you cannot measure, you cannot manage. One of the underlying problems with space management is that the data processing staff doesn't know when the problem is going to occur and doesn't know how often it occurs. This says they don't even know that it is a problem.

  When space usage is monitored, it is easy to begin to tell when space is running out. If the bus driver counts the number of passengers coming on the bus, the entry process can be stopped at the point where the last seat will be taken. The simple solutions are frequently overlooked in a highly technical area.

- *Solution 3 — Develop reorganization policies and procedures.* Good allocation of space doesn't just happen, it must be planned and worked at. The types of policies that need to be considered in the space management program include:

  - How to allocate available space among users
  - How to request more space
  - Types of organizational structures to be used for data
  - Method of charging or allocating cost of resources among users

The better run data processing organizations assign these responsibilities to the data base administrator. It is the continual reorganization of the data files that ensures the efficiency of processing, the ready availability of space, the equitable allocation of resources among users, and the indication of when additional capacity will be required.

- *Solution 4 — Utilize space management models and simulators.*
  The alternatives possible for organizing and structuring disk
  files is almost unlimited. As more users and data are involved
  in space management, the complexity increases. It takes only a
  simple understanding of mathematics to recognize that as the
  number of variables increases the combinations possible from
  those variables increase very rapidly. As the combinations
  grow, people's ability to comprehend the relationship between
  those variables diminishes.

  The solution to the proper development of sophisticated
  computer files is to use mathematical models and simulators.
  This is using the computer to help manage the computer. These
  modeling tools, or simulators, are the best friends of the data
  base administrator.

CLEANUP RULE

There is more than one way to solve a computer problem. The first
solution is almost always to buy more hardware, which is almost
always the wrong solution.

IMPEDIMENTS TO SOLVING SPACE MANAGEMENT PROBLEMS

The normal solution to a space problem is to acquire more space.
This solution when presented to management usually brings an
immediate negative reaction. The reason for this reaction is twofold:
first, the acquisition of more space is usually costly; and second, it
takes time to acquire additional space.

The specific impediments, based on the above negative management reaction, that must be overcome are:

- *Need for speed.* Unless the acquisition of space is planned over
  a period of time, it usually occurs at a crisis point: additional
  workload, special promotions, or other business activities,
  which require more space quickly. Any acceptable solution
  must normally satisfy this need for speed.

- *Effort required to implement space changes or efficiencies.* Data processing people resources may be in short supply. If those limited resources are allocated to solving space problems, they will not be available to solve other business problems. Any space management solution must identify the availability of resources to implement that solution.
- *Improperly designed application systems.* If the root of the space problem lies with inefficiently constructed application programs, the organization may not be able to spend itself out of the problem. Too frequently space solutions deal with symptoms rather than problems. Management should be convinced that proposed space problems solutions are solving the problem and not a symptom that will reappear shortly.

SPACE MANAGEMENT SURVIVAL TACTICS

Overcrowded space becomes annoying very quickly. Visualize for a moment three other people sitting in your office and more wanting to come in. You, like data processing management, will be looking for a quick solution. Some of the space management quick solutions, or survival tactics, are:

1. Break work into batches — If space is unavailable to handle the information load, that load can be broken into smaller batches and processed individually. For example, if there were too many people on the payroll to be processed, the hourly people could be processed as one batch and the management payroll as another batch.

   On-line systems require different types of batching. Because these systems are processed continuously, the needed data must be on-line at all times. Batching done in this mode would be by activity. The information being processed on a regular basis would be maintained in one batch and the dormant or very low activity records in another batch. This requires some system redesign, but in most instances it can be done relatively quickly.

2. Buy more disk drives — This is the coward's solution. It's attempting to buy your way out of a problem with money. Nothing wrong with this as a short-time survival tactic,

but if it is used to attempt to solve a more basic space problem, it may not work in the long run.
3. Reorganize the disk file — Reorganizations with limited space
   may provide only marginal processing advantages. However,
   in some cases the response time will be significantly improved
   for short periods of time. Note that this survival tactic may
   require very frequent reorganizations until a longer term
   solution can be developed.

CLEANUP RULE

Systems tend to grow, and as they grow they grow problems that
must be anticipated or the growth will stop.

12
SOLVING A COMPUTER CAPACITY PROBLEM

One hates to run out of gas on a highway. The solution appears simple. Whenever the car gets low on gas, stop and fill it up. However, there are other solutions. If the tires were better inflated or the engine better tuned, the car might not need gas as often. If gas is the major concern, a more drastic solution is to junk the current automobile and acquire a new one that is more gas-efficient. When dealing with computer capacity workloads, you must consider all solutions.

This chapter explains the considerations in computer capacity planning, both from the under- and overcapacity perspective. The symptoms of the computer running out of gas are identified, together with solutions for avoiding being stranded without enough capacity for processing. Should an emergency situation evolve, survival tactics are discussed for getting a quick burst of additional capacity.

THE COMPUTER CAPACITY PLANNING GAME

When computers were expensive and people cheap (in relation to one another), computer capacity planning was an important function. As the cost of computers began to drop, it was easier to buy too much capacity and let it sit idle until needed. After all, Parkinson would eventually fill the computer with work.

Two strong arguments can be brought forward for buying too much computer capacity. The first is that it is relatively cheap. But then one needs to ask oneself: if it were a personal computer would the it's-cheap-to-buy-overcapacity argument still hold. Second, overcapacity can be looked at like insurance. If it's ever needed, it will be there, so that the cost paid is to guarantee capacity whenever needed. A third argument is sometimes proposed, which is that because of the current high demand for computers additional hardware may not be available when the business needs it.

No argument is all onesided. There are equally strong arguments for not gorging on excess computer capacity. These arguments are: first, a planned, steady growth will be more economical than having to pay for excess capacity not needed; second, it encourages poor system development practices. If the analysts and programmers know that efficiency is unimportant because there is excess capacity, they may design inefficient systems for which the business will pay extra dollars year-in, year-out. Third, it may be interpreted as a message from management that there are plenty of dollars for data processing, which may not be the message management wants to transmit.

Earlier in the book, we talked about two characteristics of the data processing field that lead to overcapacity. These are, first, the need for professional contact, one of which is a computer hardware and software vendor. If the DP manager examines the merchandise too often, capacity impulse-buying may occur. Second is the need to use the latest devices, gadgets, and techniques. This may lead to acquiring hardware or software for personal gratification on the grounds that it will improve processing capacity.

Most computers have internal clocks that measure computer usage. There are two measures of usage. One is the number of hours that it performs useful work. This is the same principle as a taxicab. The engine may run eight hours during an eight-hour shift, but the meter that charges customers may account for only three or four hours of actual chargeable time to the customer.

Data processing management should develop charts that indicate how much of the computer capacity is being utilized. They should be further divided into the following three categories:

- Work performed by the customer that has been processed correctly the first time
- Time allocated to rerunning customer work, because it was not processed correctly the first time
- Time allocated to program development and testing and other data processing internal uses

This chart of usage should accompany any request for additional computer capacity. It doesn't take a computer expert to recognize that if the current capacity is being utilized only 40 percent of the time, there is probably little justification for additional computer capacity. Note that as the equipment approaches 70 to 80 percent of capacity, it is running at almost full capacity. This is the same concept used by economists in saying that when the unemployment rate is down to 5 percent we are running at full employment. It's not practical to expect to utilize any resource at 100 percent capacity.

SYMPTOMS OF A COMPUTER CAPACITY PROBLEM

Some people dearly love to complain. If you denied them the right to complain, you would deny them their major enjoyment in life. One must recognize that there are complaints, and there are complaints. Those complaints done for enjoyment should be ignored, and those that represent symptoms of a serious problem must be addressed. Management must be able to distinguish between the two types of symptoms.

The auditor's rule of thumb is that there must be "sufficient evidential matter" before the auditor can rely upon information provided by a third party. Lawyers shy away from relying on hearsay evidence. Valid symptoms should be supported by facts and other evidential matters. Managers can save themselves a lot of work if they ask for the facts before they begin to investigate.

The symptoms that indicate a computer capacity problem are (see Figure 43 for a list of symptoms and the severity of those symptoms):

- *Symptom 1 — Misuse of computer resources.* It is the work that is run on the computer that consumes the resources. The more efficiently the developmental process, and the more efficient the execution of those systems, the less resources required. If either the system design or the design process is grossly inefficient, excessive computer resources will be needlessly consumed. In addition, computer resources can be consumed due to personal use of the computer for games, personal projects, or work done for hire by programmers and computer operators.
- *Symptom 2 — Inadequate computer time.* Any given set of computer hardware and software is capable of running a fixed amount of work. If the work exceeds the capacity, jobs will

NO.	SYMPTOM	EXPLANATION	SEVERITY
1.	Misuse of computer resources	Computer capacity has been consumed by poor system design or excessive use of the computer for programming and testing	High
2.	Inadequate computer time	The data processing function has more work than it can perform with existing hardware and software	High
3.	Excessive response time for on-line systems	The time required for a terminal operator to get service exceeds the expected response time	High
4.	Poorly designed software	The application systems designed in-house or purchased utilize more computer resources than is normal for the type of processing involved	High
5.	Ordered hardware will not be available when needed	At the time the data processing function knew it needed hardware, it could not obtain that hardware by the needed date	Medium
6.	User complaint	Users complain about the lack of computer capacity to perform existing or new work	Medium
7.	Important projects delayed	Projects needed by users are delayed due to inadequate computer capacity to either design, test, or operate the projects	Medium
8.	Requests for additional hardware	The data processing function regularly asks for more hardware	Medium
9.	Overtime work in DP department	The data processing center computer staff must work overtime to complete the existing workload	Low

Figure 43. Symptoms of a computer capacity problem.

either be delayed or processed through other means. The lack of computer time to run the existing work is normally attributable to inadequate planning on the part of either or both the data processing function and the users.

- *Symptom 3 – Excessive response time for on-line systems.* Response time is the amount of time between the point where an individual sitting at a terminal requests service and the point where that service is supplied. The entire interactive process between the computer and a person on a terminal is a series of messages to the computer and responses from the computer. Thus, response time is not a single wait time but, rather, multiple wait periods during processing. The longer the response time, the more inefficient the terminal operator becomes. At a certain response time, the operator not only becomes inefficient, but frustrated.

  Most on-line systems promise a certain response time. This response time should be expressed in terms of average response time, with an expected service guaranteed x percent of the time. Failure to meet those response times is normally due to a lack of computer capacity.

- *Symptom 4 – Poorly designed software.* No systems designer or analyst begins with the intent of designing poor software, nor do people deliberately purchase inefficient software. However, poorly designed software can occur for any of the following reasons:

  - The efficiency of purchased software is not known at the time of purchase.
  - Programmers use inefficient programming practices.
  - Design analysts use inefficient design techniques.
  - The design and programming techniques are not synchronized with the mix of business transactions processed by the application.
  - The efficiency of the application degrades during the maintenance phase.

  It is difficult for non-data-processing people to identify inefficient software. However, the following rules of thumb give some indication of when software is inefficient:

- The processing time for a business transaction is much greater in one application than in another.
- The cost of operation of a computer far exceeds the cost estimates for that system.
- Users, data processing staff, or both openly complain about the inefficiencies of the software system.

- *Symptom 5 — Ordered hardware will not be available when needed.* One of the easiest methods to increase computer capacity is to add additional hardware. However, it is usually very specific hardware that is needed to increase capacity at an existing computer site. If the wait list for that hardware is longer than the lead time needed to increase capacity, additional hardware to upgrade current hardware will not meet a short-term need to increase computer capacity. As described in the chapter on vendor relations, hardware planning based on projected computer capacity is the preferred solution to avoid processing capacity binds.
- *Symptom 6 — User complaint.* Some symptoms are easier for managers to pick up on than others. For example, knowing that hardware will not be available may come very late in a capacity-bind situation. On the other hand, grumblings among users about inability to get their work processed may be the early signs of a forthcoming capacity bind. Lack of capacity is usually first felt at peak periods, which may be a point at which some solution may be readily available. Management should stay attuned to what users are saying and then investigate those symptoms to determine the underlying cause. For example, not getting work done may be the result of several causes, not just a capacity bind.
- *Symptom 7 — Important projects delayed.* Work in the computer center is usually prioritized. The two major categories of work are application production and application development. Normally, production takes precedence over development. Therefore, as the computer center gets into a capacity bind, development may lag due to the lack of computer time for system testing. This can result in a delay of projects that are important to the business. Again, as with other symptoms, the cause must be carefully investigated, because there are

numerous reasons projects fall behind schedule, and lack of computer capacity is only one of them.

• *Symptom 8 − Requests for additional hardware.* As previously stated, more hardware is a solution to many of the problems in data processing. It is an easy solution, because it takes very little work on the part of the computer center staff. Nevertheless, the acquisition of more hardware may be a cover-up for poor computer center practices. It is recommended that managers carefully evaluate projections and estimates of work against what's actually happening before they approve additional hardware. If the computer center is doing significantly less work than it projected, the causes may be due to poor use of existing hardware; this can be corrected at less cost than acquiring new hardware.

• *Symptom 9 − Overtime work in DP department.* The first solution to a capacity bind is to work more hours. If the work cannot be accomplished within scheduled work hours, then overtime hours can be used to complete the workload. Overtime also includes the addition of second and third shifts. These may be viable solutions, but should be studied carefully among the array of solutions available to alleviate capacity binds.

COMPUTER CAPACITY DIAGNOSTIC CHECKLIST

One of the strongest diagnostic checklists for a manager is the smell test. When things do not smell right, that is the time to conduct additional investigation. Unfortunately, to perform the smell test properly, one must have either previously smelled the stench of a mess, or have sufficient knowledge to recognize a variance from the norm.

Many senior managers have not had the opportunity to work in data processing and thus lack the experience necessary to perform the smell test. However, they can get the knowledge from any of the following means:

• Attend a vendor's executive manager workshop: Many computer vendors put on special educational sessions for senior managers. At these sessions they discuss such topics as control, organization, directing, and planning. This type of background information helps put data processing into the proper business perspective and thus helps with the smell test.

- Visit other organizations: Visiting several other similar companies to discuss their data processing is a variation of the shotgun technique. Though the visits are not directed at any specific question, they do provide insight and knowledge about data processing. They can be used as a basis of determining the variance from the norm.

- Attend a users group meeting: Many vendors of both hardware and software have organized user groups. The primary objective of these groups is to interchange technical information, but it is also a background-gathering experience. Even though much of the information presented and discussed will be beyond the technical comprehension of the senior manager, it establishes a framework of concerns that should be being addressed by that manager's own data processing function.

- Attend public seminars on managerial topics: There are many public seminars on topics that would be valuable to the senior manager. For example, the topics of audit and control, quality assurance, planning, software economics, and project management all provide the types of knowledge helpful to the manager.

With this background information, the following diagnostic checklist on computer capacity (Figure 44) will prove a valuable tool in internal investigation. This checklist is symptom-driven, with no responses being indicative of problems. For each yes response, the solution reference number pointing to the probable cause and solution (see Figure 45) should prove helpful in solving a computer capacity mystery.

COMPUTER CAPACITY PROBLEM SOLUTIONS

Lack of available computer capacity is the result of a multitude of causes. It is like an automobile stopping on a deserted road. If all automobiles stopped for a single cause, motorists could carry the solution with them. In reality, there can be a thousand causes for an automobile stopping, so that, although the symptom of the cause is known (the car stopped), the solution to the problem may be difficult and costly to determine.

NO.	CAUSE OF PROBLEM		PRINCIPLE VIOLATED	RECOMMENDED SOLUTION	
	SPECIFIC	GENERAL		GENERAL	SPECIFIC
1	Level of computer operations performance not known	Noncompliance, ineffective	Compliance	Comply, revise	Establish performance standards and monitor compliance
2	Outside hardware/software requests are always on an emergency basis	Poor sequence	Smooth flow	Rearrange	Develop capacity growth plans
3	Users are not concerned with EDP costs	Complicated, costly	Noncompliance, ineffective	Comply, revise	Initiate a charge-out system
4	Additional hardware is needed for peak periods only	Complicated, costly	Noncompliance, ineffective	Comply, revise	Use service bureau for peak periods

Figure 45. Computer capacity problem solution matrix.

Lack of computer capacity is a very prominent symptom of computer problems. It occurs over and over again in most installations. Also, because of the increasing demand for computer capacity the symptom recurs like an unwanted friend.

Organizations have found four basic solutions to controlling the growth of a computer. The objective of these solutions is not to stop computer growth, but rather to control it, to be assured that there is an associated benefit with the cost of increased capacity.

The four most popular solutions to controlling computer capacity are:

- *Solution 1 — Establish performance standards, and monitor compliance.* Until some level of performance standard has been adopted, there is no way to tell the efficiency or inefficiency of applications using computer resources. It is easy to single out an application, but without standards it is hard to state that the system was not built properly, because there are no construction standards, nor operated efficiently, because there are no operational standards to measure against. The type of performance standards that help optimize operating efficiency are:

  - Compilation and test time standards
  - File accessing standards
  - Programming and file organizational standards
  - Documentation standards

- *Solution 2 — Develop capacity growth plans.* Unplanned computer growth is generally uneconomical computer growth. The planning may be done at the convenience of the computer vendor — in other words vendors offer bargains that can't be refused — or at emergency times when a premium may be paid for quick installation and operation. A well-planned data processing function is normally an economically run data processing function. As discussed in earlier chapters, the plan should be both short-range (i.e., one year) and long-range (three to five years).

- *Solution 3 — Initiate a charge-out system.* In the early stages of computer usage, the growth rate can appear on a graph like a rocket heading up to an earth orbit. One company projected during the early years of its data processing function that, if the growth rate continued for eight years, the company would be spending more on data processing than it would be receiving from sales.

The solution to many companies' growth rates is to make users accountable for the resources they consume. This requires the data processing department to keep records on use of resources and then to charge the users through an internal budgetary process for those costs. If the company does not have a budgetary system, the cost can still be easily calculated and published. Most systems have computer software than can calculate these charges for minimal cost. Sometimes when users see what a certain change or system costs, they recognize alternative means of accomplishing the same work for lesser cost. Sometimes when senior management sees the cost associated with data processing, it orders solutions for apparent misuses of computer resources.

- *Solution 4 – Use service bureau for peak periods.* Organizations that run computer systems in-house sometimes look only at in-house solutions for their work. There is nothing wrong with occasionally taking peak-load work and running it in another installation. This can be done by contract or as the need exists.

  If work is going to be run off-site, some preplanning must be done. At a minimum, it will involve ensuring that the organization's applications are runnable on a service center. This normally means that the interfaces be properly established. Normally this, and a general working agreement with the service center, can be established at no cost to the business. Then when capacity binds are occurring, the installation quickly can shift work to the service center and have it performed and returned in almost the same time it would have taken in-house.

  Obviously, on-line systems cannot be as easily shifted. Still, some hotel reservation systems use this concept by switching calls to a secondary backup system at a service center at any time during the day. With some on-line systems, the batch background work can be shifted, freeing more on-line capacity. Knowing the desirable solution, DP analysts can usually work out the methods.

CLEANUP RULE

A good computer plan worked out in advance is far better than a perfect computer plan unavailable at the time of need.

IMPEDIMENTS TO PROVIDING NEEDED COMPUTER CAPACITY

Even the best plans of men are frequently hampered by happenstance. Most data processing managers recognize the need for a continually increasing computer resource. In addition, most data processing managers want bigger and more powerful computer installations. The impediment usually lies outside the data processing function.

The three major impediments to having the needed computer capacity when needed are:

- *No logical upward step.* Sometimes businesses reach the upper end of a line or family of computers. For example, the accelerator is pressed to the floor, but the car still won't go as fast as the driver wants. Once engine capacity has reached maximum, the only way the driver can go faster is to get another car. This is not an easy step, and it may be difficult to take. In some instances, many computer systems will need to be rewritten before a new family of computers can be installed. Note that most computer vendors make it easy for their customers to acquire more hardware until they reach the upper end of a line of computers. At this point, conversion becomes costly.
- *Lack of budget.* Additional hardware and software cost funds. If those funds are not available or will not become available, the equipment cannot be obtained. Note that to place a holding order for equipment does not cost anything, but once the equipment is installed the costs begin. This impediment is easy to recognize, but may be hard to overcome.
- *Unwillingness to stand up to dominant users.* The computer resources are consumed by the users of those resources. It is not unusual for one or two users to monopolize the computer resources. In many instances, that can be a limited number of

individuals. This is particularly true when there is not a charge-out cost for the use of those services.

If either data processing or senior management does not force those users to curtail their use of services, computer capacity is quickly consumed. The addition of more hardware may be only a very short-term solution to this dilemma, as the more capacity available, the more jobs those dominant users can perform on the computer.

COMPUTER CAPACITY SURVIVAL TACTICS

Organizations can rarely just stop processing. When there is more work than computer capacity, solutions must be found to the predicament. The most common methods of surviving a computer capacity bind are:

1. Operate more hours — Fortunately, there are twenty-four hours a day, and seven days a week. Until those hours have been consumed, there is still more capacity, assuming that the hardware can remain operational. Although people may not like working weekends or the graveyard shift at night, these are solutions.

    Some of the more palatable ways of making extra hours more enticing to the computer center staff are:

    — Three twelve-hour shifts: This enables people to finish their work week in three days of twelve-hour shifts. There is little time for enjoyment during those twelve hours, but, because the individual has four days off, it is frequently a very desirable position.
    — Overtime pay: Paying people shift differentials or over-time pay helps compensate for personal inconvenience.
    — More supervisory positions: The more hours the computer center runs, the more openings for supervisors, and thus a greater opportunity to advance.

2. Optimize current workload and mix of work — These solutions require the computer center to take a hard look at both the work it is running and the schedule for running that work. There are many software aids that can optimize programs,

using such tools as COBOL optimizers, as well as software packages that can determine the best mix of work to get the maximum throughput out of the computer. This solution normally is a labor-intensive solution used to overcome a hardware capacity problem.

3. Prioritize work — The high-priority work may be delayed due to being intermixed with low-priority work. In some instances, work may be being performed to optimize systems in which the optimization process uses more resources than will be saved by the reduced operating time. In other instances, users request changes that could be delayed or special runs that could be performed manually or done without. Normally, this solution requires senior management involvement, because it requires telling users the work they want will not be performed or will not be performed at the time they want it performed.

CLEANUP RULE

The course of least resistance is often the road to the scrap heap. Obtaining additional computer capacity may require biting the bullet on inefficient operating and computer usage practices.

Part 3
Avoiding Problems in the Future

If you must make a mistake, let it be a new one. Investigating the cause of each computer defect and putting a solution into use has the long-term effect of minimizing problems.

13
AVOIDING THE RECURRENCE OF
A COMPUTER MESS

People who have been in automobile accidents tend to wear their seat belts thereafter. In general, people who have experienced serious problems take great measures to avoid the recurrence of those problems. Likewise, managers who have gotten caught in a computer mess may never want it to happen again. What must be avoided is throwing the baby out with the bath water, so that the solution to the mess is not more painful than the mess itself.

Eradicating a computer mess in a manner that will prevent its recurrence is a long-term process. It would not be unusual for a business to take eighteen to thirty-six months to turn around a problem computer installation. Fortunately, the method for doing it is known.

This chapter provides a four-step plan of action for senior management to turn around a troubled data processing function. The steps are easy in principle and work in practice. The key ingredient to making the plan work is "management backbone." Often the short-term solutions appear more desirable because they appear to offer a quick turnaround. Unfortunately, they are just that — short-term solutions.

THE PLAN OF ACTION TO ERADICATE COMPUTER MESSES

Eradicating a computer mess must start with senior management. Information is a resource of the organization and thus should be managed like any other resource. Senior management must initiate the policies that require the management of that information.

The four-step plan of action is listed below, and then the steps are individually explained:

- *Step 1 — Establish an EDP quality policy.* This step requires management to state the level of quality it expects from information processing.

- *Step 2 − Appoint someone in charge.*   Policies come to fruition only when a single individual is charged with the responsibility of making them work.
- *Step 3 − Establish a quality assurance function.*   This is the function responsible for the proper functioning of the information processing process.
- *Step 4 − Establish a quality control function.*   Quality control needs to be practiced in the development and operation of individual application systems.   This is the function that ensures that the products produced by the data processing function meet the standards established in management's quality policy.

STEP 1 − ESTABLISH AN EDP QUALITY POLICY

One of the major challenges to senior management is to raise dramatically the quality of products and services offered.   One of the major services of many businesses is information processing.   The way to achieve an increase in the quality of data processing is to implement quality improvement activities throughout the organization.

Quality data processing is everybody's responsibility.   It is the responsibility of the users, the data processing personnel, and senior management.   However, the initial emphasis for quality must come from senior management.

A quality policy is senior management's statement of what it expects from its information processing function.   Information processing is used in lieu of data processing because it is a companywide consideration, and not a single departmental consideration, although the data processing function will have the burden of implementing much of the policy.

A data processing quality policy should make the following five basic points:

1. Quality of information processing is a cornerstone of the organization − Without quality information, few other aspects of the business will be able to produce quality products.
2. The objective of the quality policy is to provide information products and services that are defect-free − The users and originators of those services must define the standards of

performance for which the processing objectives will then be to meet those standards and eradicate defects (i.e., variances from standards).

3. Each individual involved in information processing must learn to do things right the first time — Training in performance must be an integral part of quality data processing. It is also an attitudinal approach that must be instilled by management and coupled with the appropriate tools to let people know whether or not they are performing the job properly. This involves both assuring that the best possible process is developed and that people can determine whether or not they are following that process properly.

4. Each stage of the process must be defect-free — In other words, quality cannot be built in after the fact, but must be built in during the developmental process. Not only must products be defect-free, but the assurance of the defect-free product must occur throughout the developmental life cycle.

5. Quality is truly everyone's job — Though a single individual will be accountable for implementing a quality policy, that individual is not responsible for quality. Unless all are responsible for the quality of their own work, it will not happen.

STEP 2 — APPOINT SOMEONE IN CHARGE

It would be unusual to talk to any manager, any data processing professional, or any user and find that they do not favor quality information processing. It would be equally unusual to find any systems analyst or programmer who deliberately starts out to build a poor-quality system. The problem with quality is not that people do not want it; the problem is that there are many different pressures, and quality is only one of them.

When people are assigned to build a computer application, they face four pressures, as follows:

- Pressure 1 — Installing the specified requirements
- Pressure 2 — Installing the requirements on the scheduled date
- Pressure 3 — Installing the requirements within the allotted budget
- Pressure 4 — Meeting the application quality standards

The first three pressures normally take precedence over the fourth. As budgets run short, as the scheduled implementation date approaches, or as requirements change, tradeoffs are made with quality. The more common tradeoffs include:

- Tradeoff 1 — Perform fewer system tests
- Tradeoff 2 — Meet less with the users to fully define requirements
- Tradeoff 3 — Create less system documentation
- Tradeoff 4 — Create less documentation explaining to the user how to use the system
- Tradeoff 5 — Do less training of systems and user personnel

These tradeoffs enable the system to be completed on time, within budget, and they satisfy the major stated requirements. What they may not permit is the elimination of defects, the creation of an easy-to-maintain system, the creation of any easy-to-use system, or the inclusion of the niceties that make the system work well.

The U.S. automotive industry experienced these problems in the 1960s and 1970s. The companies prided themselves on completing an automobile every forty-seven seconds, even if the doors didn't close properly, the panels didn't meet correctly, and some parts didn't work properly. The overriding goal was to complete the car within the schedule and worry about the quality later. Any defects in factory quality were believed to be correctable at the local dealership. The local dealer, not having a lot of time, let the purchaser of the automobile uncover the defects and bring it back for correction. The net result was that the perceived and actual quality of U.S. automobiles nosedived, which may have caused an irrevocable decline in confidence and sales of U.S. automobiles.

The same concept can occur in any data processing function. Once quality is damaged, the confidence in data processing and the credibility of that function may likewise nosedive. The alternate solution for many users is to contract their work with outside groups or to acquire small computers and perform the computer processing themselves.

The reason for much of the decline in quality is that a high-level individual has not been appointed responsible to ensure that quality occurs. Most quality control inspectors are very low-level individuals with minimal clout. When they complain too much, they are replaced, or cosmetic corrections are made, and the product sent out to the marketplace. When quality is moved up to a high enough level in an organization that it becomes visible, action is taken.

STEP 3 – ESTABLISH A QUALITY ASSURANCE FUNCTION

Quality assurance is sometimes referred to as the quality control of quality control. It is the group responsible for the process, not the product. Quality control is charged with evaluating the process to produce the products, to ensure that the process is a viable and reliable process. Quality assurance recommendations are directed at improving the process, not improving the product.

It is highly possible that everyone in the information processing area can be performing their work correctly, but still producing poor-quality products. If a carpenter attempted to make a close-fitting joint using an axe to cut the wood, it would be rare that the joint would ever fit well. It wouldn't matter how carefully the carpenter attempted to cut the wood with the axe, it would be difficult to perform or create a high-quality joint.

Many data processing functions face that same situation. They have neither the tools nor approaches that give them a high probability of producing a quality data processing system. It is the quality assurance function that will evaluate the process and change it where necessary.

Experience has shown us which practices work and which do not. We can express these as computer practices, or processes, that have associated with them a high risk. High risk means that the probability of being successful is low. Some computer practices however, offer very low risk. This means that when the low-risk practices are used, there is a much higher probability that a quality computer system will be produced.

The U.S. General Accounting Office commissioned a study of federal systems to indicate for the significant system characteristics the practices that were indicative of high, medium, and low risk. These practices are provided in Figure 46.

The use of this figure is as follows:

1. Locate the significant characteristic of interest – The figure includes both general and application characteristics. For

SIGNIFICANT CHARACTERISTICS	INDICATIVE OF HIGH RISK	INDICATIVE OF MEDIUM RISK	INDICATIVE OF LOW RISK
System scope and complexity			
a) Organizational breadth			
1. Important functions	Must meet important conflicting needs of several organizational units	Meets limited conflicting requirements of cooperative organizational units	No significant conflicting needs, serves primarily one organizational unit
2. Unrelated organizational units deeply involved	Dependent upon data flowing from many organizational units not under unified direction	Dependent upon data from a few organizational units with a common interest, if not unified control	Virtually all input data comes from a small group of sections under unified control
b) Data processing breadth			
1. Number of transaction types	More than 25	6 to 25	Fewer than 6
2. Number of related record segments	More than 6	4 to 6	Fewer than 4
3. Output reports	More than 20	10 to 20	Fewer than 10
c) Margin of error (necessity for everything to work perfectly, for "split-second timing," for great cooperation (perhaps including external parties), etc.)	Very demanding	Realistically demanding	Comfortable margin
Technical complexity	*High, aggressive*	*Moderate*	*Conservative*
a) Number of programs, including sort/merge	More than 35	20 to 35	Fewer than 20
b) Programming approach (number of module/functions interacting with an update/file maintenance program)	More than 20	10 to 20	Fewer than 10
c) Size of largest program	More than 60K	25K to 60K	Fewer than 25K
d) Adaptability of program to change	Low, due to monolithic program design	Can surmount problems with adequate talent and effort	Relatively high; program straightforward, modular, roomy, relatively unpatched, well documented, etc.

Figure 46. Computer practices appendix.*

SIGNIFICANT CHARACTERISTICS	INDICATIVE OF HIGH RISK	INDICATIVE OF MEDIUM RISK	INDICATIVE OF LOW RISK
e) Relationship to equipment in use	Pushes equipment capacity near limits	Within capacities	Substantial unused capacity
f) Reliance on on-line data-entry automatic document reading or other advanced techniques	Heavy, including direct entry of transactions and other changes into the master files	Remote-batch processing under remote operations control	None or limited to file inquiry
Pioneering aspects (extent to which the system applies new, difficult, and unproven techniques on a broad scale or in a new situation, thus placing great demands on —the non-EDP departments, —systems and programming groups, —EDP operations personnel, —customers or vendors, etc.)	*Aggressively pioneering* More than a few relatively untried equipment or system software components or system techniques or objectives, at least one of which is crucial	*Moderate* Few untried systems components and their functions are moderately important; few, if any pioneering system objectives and techniques	*Conservative* No untried system components, no pioneering system objectives or techniques
System stability	*Unstable, much is new*	*Moderate change, most is not new*	*Stable, little is new*
a) Age of system (since inception or last big change)	Less than 1 year	1 to 2 years	Over 2 years
b) Frequency of significant change	More than 4 per year	2 to 4 per year	Fewer than 2 per year
c) Extent of total change in last year	Affecting more than 25% of programs	Affecting 10 to 25% of programs	Affecting less than 10% of programs
d) User approval of specifications	Cursory, essentially uninformed	Reasonably informed as to general but not detailed specifications; approval apt to be informal	Formal, written approval, based on informed judgment and written, reasonably precise specifications
Satisfaction of user requirements	*Low satisfaction, many problems*	*Reasonable satisfaction, some problems*	*High satisfaction*
a) Completeness	Incomplete, significant number of items not processed in proper period	Occasional problems but normally no great difficulties	No significant data omitted or processed in wrong period

Figure 46. Computer practices appendix* (cont.).

SIGNIFICANT CHARACTERISTICS	INDICATIVE OF HIGH RISK	INDICATIVE OF MEDIUM RISK	INDICATIVE OF LOW RISK
b) Accuracy	Considerable error problem, with items in suspense or improperly handled	Occasional problems, but normally no great difficulties	Errors not numerous or of consequence
c) Promptness in terms of needs	Reports and documents delayed so as to be almost useless; forced to rely on informal records	Reports and documents not always available when desired; present timetable inconvenient but tolerable	Reports and documents produced soon enough to meet operational needs
d) Accessibility of details (to answer inquiries, review for reasonableness, make corrections, etc.)	Great difficulty in obtaining details of transactions or balances except with much delay	Complete details available monthly; in interim, details available with some difficulty and delay	Details readily available
e) Reference to source documents (audit trail)	Great difficulty in locating documents promptly	Audit trail excellent; some problems with filing and storage	Audit trail excellent; filing and storage good
f) Conformity with established system specifications	Actual procedures and operations differ in important respects	Limited tests indicate that actual procedures and operations differ in only minor respects and operations produce desired results	Limited tests indicate actual procedures and operations produce desired results
Source data origin and approval	*Leaves much to be desired*	*Reasonable*	*Sound procedures, well carried out*
a) People, procedures, knowledge, discipline, division of duties, etc., in departments that —originate data —approve data	Situation leaves much to be desired	Situation satisfactory, but could stand some improvement	Situation satisfactory
b) Data control procedures outside the EDP organization	None or relatively ineffective; e.g., use of noncritical fields, loose liaison with EDP department, little concern with rejected items	Control procedures based on noncritical fields; reasonably effective liaison with EDP department	Control procedures include critical fields; good tie-in with EDP department; especially good on rejected items
c) Error rate	Over 7% of transactions rejected after leaving source data department	4–7% of transactions rejected after leaving source data department	Less than 4% of transactions rejected after leaving source data department
d) Error backlog	Many 30-day-old items	Mostly 10–15-day-old items	Items primarily less than 7 days old

Figure 46. Computer practices appendix* (cont).

SIGNIFICANT CHARACTERISTICS	INDICATIVE OF HIGH RISK	INDICATIVE OF MEDIUM RISK	INDICATIVE OF LOW RISK
Input data control (within EDP department)	*Leaves much to be desired*	*Reasonable*	*Sound, well-executed*
a) Relationship with external controls	Loose liaison with external control units; little concern with rejected items; batch totals not part of input procedures; only use controls like item counts; no control totals of any kind	Reasonably effective liaison with external data control units; good control over new items, but less satisfactory control over rejected items; batch totals not received, but generated by computer	Good tie-in with external control units for both valid and rejected items; batch totals received as part of input process
b) Selection of critical control fields	Control based on non-critical fields	Control based on a mixture of critical and non-critical fields, with effective supplementary checks	Control established on critical fields
c) Controls over key transcription	Control based on batch totals	Control based on transmittal sheets; batch totals and key verification of critical fields not batch-controlled	Control based on transmittal sheets, batch totals maintained on data logs, key verification of all critical fields, and written "signoff" procedures
Data validation (computer editing)	*Few, relatively simple tests*	*Reasonably effective tests*	*Extensive, well-designed tests*
a) Edit tests	Alpha-numeric tests	Range and alpha-tests	Range, alpha-numeric, and check-digit tests
b) Sophistication	Simple, based on edit of one field at a time	Simple editing plus some editing based on the interrelationship of two	Simple editing plus extensive edit tests based on the interrelationship of two or more fields
c) Application to critical data	A considerable amount of critical data is not edited.	A few critical fields are edited only indirectly	Editing performed on critical fields
d) Error balancing, retrieval, and correction procedures	Error rejected by system and eliminated from controls; treated as new items when reintroduced	Number and value of rejected items carried in suspense account without electronically maintained details	Error carried in suspense account in total and in detail until removed by correction
Computer processing control	*Limited—excessive reliance on manual procedure*	*Reasonable*	*Comprehensive and automatic*
a) Controls within machine room	Informal operating instructions	Written operating procedures	Operations are based on a schedule, use up-to-date instructions

Figure 46. Computer practices appendix* (cont).

SIGNIFICANT CHARACTERISTICS	INDICATIVE OF HIGH RISK	INDICATIVE OF MEDIUM RISK	INDICATIVE OF LOW RISK
b) Manual and electronic safeguards against incorrect processing of files	Tape library controls by serial number; no programmed checks	Tape library controls by serial number; programmed checks applied to file identification	Programmed label check applied to serial number, experiation date, and file identification
c) Recording of run-to-run debit, credit, and balance totals for both transaction processing and master file records	Run-to-run totals not used	Run-to-run totals printed and compared manually	Run-to-run totals printed and compared by program
d) Documentation status	Poor or no standards; uneven adherence; not part of system and program development	Adequate practices not uniformly adhered to; documentation done after the fact	Excellent standards closely adhered to and carried out as part of system and program development
e) System test practices	Some transaction paths not tested	Each transaction path tested individually	Each transaction path tested in combination with all other transactions
Output control	*Essentially lacking*	*Reasonable*	*Good in EDP and user department*
a) Quantitative controls —in EDP department	Virtually nonexistent	Hard to tie back meaningfully to input controls	Tied back to input controls
—in user department	Virtually nonexistent	Hard to tie back meaningfully to input controls	Tied back to input controls
b) Qualitative controls	Documents and reports accepted virtually without review	Sample documents and reports receive limited review	Documents and reports tested in detail, in addition to receiving a common sense review of reasonable data limits
c) Distribution controls	No routine report distribution procedures	Routine procedures for distribution limited to list of users and frequency of report delivery.	Written procedures requiring that control log indicate receipt by user, time of action, accounting for each copy, etc.

Figure 46. Computer practices appendix* (cont.).

SIGNIFICANT CHARACTERISTICS	INDICATIVE OF HIGH RISK	INDICATIVE OF MEDIUM RISK	INDICATIVE OF LOW RISK
On-line processing controls			
a) Data transmission controls, including —error detection —error recovery —data security	The front-end control program does not validate operator identification codes or messages sequence number and does not send acknowledgment to origin	The front-end control program checks terminal and operator identification codes and messages sequence number, sends acknowledgment to origin, and provides a transaction log	The front-end control program validates terminal/operator identification codes plus transaction authorization codes and message sequence number and count, corrects errors, sends acknowledgment to origin, and provides log of transactions plus copies of updated master file records
b) Data validation controls, including error detection and correction	Neither the front-end control nor the application processing program checks for authorization approval codes; no check digits are used with identification keys; there is little use of extensive data relationship tests; erroneous transactions are rejected without analysis or suspense entry	The application program checks approval codes for key transaction types only, but check digits are not used with identification keys; extensive data relationship tests are used; erroneous transactions are sent back to terminal with a note, but no suspense entry is made	The application program validates approval codes for all transactions, and check digits are used with identification keys; data relationship tests are used extensively; erroneous transactions are noted in error suspense file when sent back to terminal with note
c) Data processing controls, including —error detection —transaction processing controls —master file processing controls —file recovery provisions	Application program produces a total number of transactions processed; no master file processing controls; file recovery provisions limited to periodic copy of master file	Application program produces a summary record of all debit and credit transactions processed; no master file processing controls; file recovery provisions limited to transaction log and periodic copy of master file	Stored validation range values are used to validate transaction fields; application program summarizes all transactions processed by type, with credit and debit values for each terminal, and uses a master file control trailer record that is balanced by program routine; end-of-processing file recovery provisions include transaction log of active master file records.

*Based on studies by the U.S. General Accounting Office.

Figure 46. Computer practices appendix* (cont.).

example, the first part of Figure 46 talks about the organizational breadth covered by the application (i.e., a general characteristic). The last characteristic discussed in the figure is on-line processing controls, which is a very specific application characteristic. To review the development process or a specific application, all applicable characteristics would be reviewed individually.

2. Identify the risk characteristics — For each significant characteristic the figure indicates the criteria that result in a high, medium, or low risk. For example, the first characteristic addressed in Figure 46 is the important functions included within the system as a subset of organizational breadth. If the functions included within a particular application system "must meet important conflicting needs of several organizational units," then that system is a high-risk system. If there are "no significant conflicting needs, serves primarily one organizational unit," however, then the application can be considered a low-risk application.

3. Accumulate level of risk — After all the appropriate characteristics have been examined, the user of Figure 46 should indicate how many of the characteristics are high-risk, how many are medium-risk, and how many are low-risk. This risk profile, if skewed toward low-risk, will indicate a low-risk application, and if it is skewed toward high-risk will indicate a potential or actual high-risk application.

The low-risk indicators can be used by quality assurance in the development of a low-risk process. If the process is designed to build systems that have the low-risk characteristics, then that process is highly likely to produce low-risk applications.

STEP 4 — ESTABLISH A QUALITY CONTROL FUNCTION

The objective of quality control is to ensure that only quality products are produced. This requires first that quality be defined, and second that the developers of systems be provided the tools to enable them to assess the quality of the products they build and operate.

Quality control is best performed by the group that develops and operates the computer systems. The quality policy principle that says that quality is everybody's responsibility means that the responsibility for quality must reside in each individual. A poor policy is to make one individual responsible for building a product and another responsible for ensuring that the quality is in the product. Both responsibilities should occur with the same individual.

Examples of quality control tools for a data processing function include:

- Critical success criteria — The predefinition of the criteria that are critical to the success of the project, so that projects can be measured by the achievement of those criteria.
- Developmental process self-checklists — These checklists indicate all the practices that should be followed in the development of a project, so that the developers can evaluate whether or not they have performed all the necessary steps.
- EDP standard self-assessment checklist — A checklist for project personnel to use in determining whether or not they have compiled with all the necessary standards of the data processing department.
- Schedules and budgets — Targets to meet in either dates or dollars in building or operating a computer system.
- Test decks — A series of transactions to be used in evaluating a computer system. The system must process the test transactions correctly before it is entered into a production status.

The occurrence of the symptoms described in Chapters 3 through 12 indicates lack of quality. The symptoms do not indicate what is wrong, but they do indicate that a potential problem has occurred. Therefore, an understanding of the symptoms can be used in a quality control manner. If these symptoms are continually being evaluated, as soon as one of the symptoms appears, an immediate investigation can be undertaken to catch a potential defect at the point it occurs.

The list of symptoms can be used in the same manner as an annual medical examination. The doctor will look for all sorts of symptoms and, if none are found, will pronounce the patient in good health. If a symptom is found, however, such as high blood pressure or above-normal temperature, then the doctor must do additional diagnosis to determine the cause.

NO.	SYMPTOM OF A COMPUTER MESS	PRESENT YES	PRESENT NO	COMMENTS	3	4	5	6	7	8	9	10	11	12
												CHAPTER ADDRESSING SOLUTION		
1.	Over budget				X	X	X		X	X				
2.	Behind schedule				X	X	X		X	X				
3.	High turnover in EDP				X					X				
4.	Inadequate computer time				X	X							X	X
5.	Excessive computer time				X	X	X		X					
6.	Inability of staff to diagnose cause of problem				X			X						
7.	Out-of-balance reports										X			
8.	Errors in computer output										X			
9.	Input data lost							X			X	X	X	
10.	Input data wrong							X			X			
11.	Processing incorrect								X	X	X	X	X	
12.	Files lost											X		
13.	Output data lost										X			
14.	User uninformed of change						X			X				
15.	EDP uninformed of change				X		X							

Figure 47. Computer mess symptoms checklist.

NO.	SYMPTOM OF A COMPUTER MESS	PRESENT YES	PRESENT NO	COMMENTS	3	4	5	6	7	8	9	10	11	12
					CHAPTER ADDRESSING SOLUTION									
16.	Unassigned responsibility				X			X						
17.	Important projects delayed				X		X							X
18.	No one accepts responsibility for problem					X	X	X		X				
19.	Vendor contract dispute					X								
20.	Needed services for a product not provided by the contract					X			X					
21.	Purchased application requires extensive in-house modification					X								
22.	Ordered hardware will not be available when needed					X								X
23.	Manual adjustments made to computer outputs						X				X		X	
24.	Excessive change requests to system						X							
25.	Changes required on short notice						X				X			
26.	Duplicate records maintained by user						X				X			
27.	Abnormal termination (hang-up)								X				X	
28.	Terminal lock-up							X			X		X	
29.	User complaint							X			X			X
30.	Customer complaint							X						

Figure 47. Computer mess symptoms checklist (cont.).

NO.	SYMPTOM OF A COMPUTER MESS	PRESENT YES	PRESENT NO	COMMENTS	CHAPTER ADDRESSING SOLUTION 3	4	5	6	7	8	9	10	11	12
31.	System abuse for personal gain							X				X		
32.	System abuse—unintentional							X				X		
33.	Unmaintainable code								X	X				
34.	Startup/conversion error								X		X			
35.	Misuse of computer resources								X	X		X		X
36.	EDP does not understand business needs									X				
37.	Dispute between EDP personnel and user									X				
38.	Lack of backup data											X		
39.	Excessive time to recover											X		
40.	Requests for additional hardware												X	X
41.	Overtime work in DP department											X	X	X
42.	Excessive response time for on-line systems												X	X
43.	Poorly designed software												X	X

Figure 47. Computer mess symptoms checklist (cont.).

The Computer Mess Symptoms Checklist (Figure 47) is to be used as a periodic evaluation of the computer system. Each computer project should be evaluated against a list of symptoms. The checklist is designed to indicate whether the symptom is present or not. If it is present, then the chapter or chapters addressing that solution should be consulted. The chapters will provide sufficient insight on determining the cause of the symptom and recommending solutions. This checklist can be used whenever there is a managerial concern about the viability of a computer system or project.

ACTION IS THE KEY INGREDIENT

Knowing problems and identifying solutions are only part of the answer. Many people think that all that is needed is to identify the cause of the problem and recommend the solution. That is only one step. The second, and sometimes the more important, step is sustaining action in order to be effective. Too frequently action ceases before the solution is properly implemented. It takes determination and stamina to maintain action clear through the analysis and implementation process.

There is no greater finale to man's effort to clean up a computer mess than the simple words, "It is done."

INDEX

INDEX